# SCIENTIFICA
# HERMETICA

## An Introduction to the Science of Alchemy

**Vae Vae Vae
to you Sophists.**

**Ouinta Essentia.**

Contents: Part 1) Introduction to the Gnosis of the Nature of
All Things; The Nature of all Motion; The Nature of Space;
The Mover; The Bodiless; The Divine Essence; The Essence
of God; The Nature of the Father. Part 2) The Sacred Sermon
of Hermes; The Text; God, Godhead, Godly Nature; The Birth
of the Cyclic Gods; The Work of the Cyclic Gods.

# A.S Raleigh

ISBN 1-56459-492-0

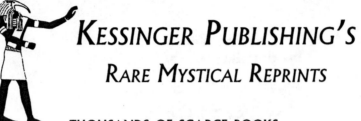

# DEDICATION

To that faithful body of students scattered throughout the world—who have ever devoted themselves to the Quest for the Gnosis of the Mind—this course of Lessons on Hermetic Science is lovingly dedicated, with the hope that it may in some degree aid them on their way, and may in some small measure be the means of leading them into the Old, Old Path of Devotion joined with the Gnosis.

THE AUTHOR.

# CONTENTS

## INTRODUCTORY NOTE

In the Hermetic Writing there are two accounts of the origin of the Kosmos. These two are given in The Shepherd of Men and in the Sacred Sermon. While there seem to be discrepancies in the two, there are really none. The Shepherd of Men is the Religious Version, while the Sacred Sermon is the Scientific Version of the same events, and hence, being written from two distinct standpoints, they deal with the subject from different angles, and hence one gives matters that are eliminated from the other. In the Author's Commentary on the Shepherd of Men the Religious Doctrine is given, and in these Lessons the Scientific Doctrine is given. No one has been able to interpret the Sacred Sermon for the reason that it is one of the most condensed of all the Sacred accounts. There has never been a single account of the Genesis of the Universe that was complete, or that could be understood without the Esoteric Key. We have four such accounts, the one in Genesis, the one in the Stanzas of Dzjn, the one in the Shepherd of Men and the one in the Sacred Sermon. They must all be studied comparatively in order to understand them correctly. But in any event, one must have the Esoteric Key to each if he would grasp their meaning. In these lessons, we propose to give you the Esoteric Key to two of these accounts of the Creation.

In the Introduction to the Gnosis of the Nature of All Things, we have the basic principles of the scientific relation of all things in their ultimate nature. No one without this information can possibly understand the basic principles of Hermetic Science. Any one who undertakes to delve into the mysteries of Hermetic Science without this Key will be doomed to failure from the start. But with the key to the Gnosis of the Nature of all things, and the Key to the Genesis of the Universe as given in these Lessons, one will have no difficulty whatsoever in understanding those principles. Of course he can make little out of this Initiation into Hermetic Science without first having mastered our Lessons in Hermetic Philosophy, which should precede the study of Hermetic Science.

Long before the time of the First Hermes, there existed an Esoteric Order devoted to the study of these subjects. In the course of time the Key was lost, and as a result, the Great Wisdom was in danger of departing from the earth. At this time, the First Hermes was born in Atlantis. He was the first to give the Books of Hermes to the Brotherhood. From this time on there was the definite statement of the Great Truths of Hermetic Philosophy, Hermetic Science, Hermetic Art and the Hidden Wisdom. In the course of time the same race settled in Egypt, and after the sinking of Atlantis, all communication between the parent Order and the Egyptian Section was broken off, and then as the language was changed, in time the true Key as well as the Sacred Text was lost. The Second Hermes, a little over ten thousand years ago gave the Teaching a second time. This remained pure for five thousand years, when at last it was lost again. At this time the Third Hermes appeared, and gave the Brotherhood the Teaching for the third time. Since that time the Brotherhood has perpetuated it down to date. These lessons are the official declaration of the Brotherhood as to the Esoteric Meaning of the

Teaching relative to Hermetic Science, just as our Philosophia Hermetica was the official declaration as to the meaning of Hermetic Philosophy and its Esoteric side. In view of these facts, let our students read first Philosophia Hermetica, and then Scientifica Hermetica, and after having mastered the two courses of lessons, they will be in a position to undertake the study of the Hermetic Art. These three courses will fit them for the study of Alchemy.

We wish to call their attention to the fact that these lessons are in every sense of the word Official and Authoritative, and represent the Esoteric Instructions of the Brotherhood on these subjects. The reason why this Esoteric Knowledge is now being given to the world will be readily understood by those who know the nature of the Cycle in which we live at this time.

A. S. RALEIGH.

Chicago, Ill., April 1, 1916.

# Scientifica Hermetica

## An Introduction to the Gnosis of the Nature of All Things

---

### TEXT

Parthey (G.) *Hermetis Trismegisti Poemander* (Berlin, 1854), 19-30.

Patrizzi (F.) *Nova de Universis Philosophia* (Venice, 1593), 18-20.

Mead (G. R. S.) *Thrice Greatest Hermes* (London, 1906). Corpus Hermeticum II (III).

1. *Hermes.* All that is moved, Asclepius, is it not moved *in* something and *by* something?

*Asclepius.* Assuredly.

*Her.* And must not that in which it's moved be greater than the moved?

*Asc.* It must.

*Her.* Mover, again, has greater power than moved?

*Asc.* It has, of course.

*Her.* The nature, furthermore, of that in which it's moved must be quite other from the nature of the moved?

*Asc.* It must completely.

2. *Her.* Is not, again, this cosmos vast [so

vast], that than it there exists no body greater?

*Asc.* Assuredly.

*Her.* And massive too, for it is crammed with multitudes of other mighty frames, nay rather all the other bodies that there are?

*Asc.* It is.

*Her.* And yet the cosmos is a body?

*Asc.* It is a body.

*Her.* And one that's moved?

3. *Asc.* Assuredly.

*Her.* Of what size, then, must be the space in which it's moved; and of what kind [must be] the nature [of that space]? Must it not be far vaster [than the cosmos] in order that it may be able to find room for its continued course, so that the moved may not be cramped for want of room and lose its motion?

*Asc.* Something, Thrice-greatest one, it needs must be, immensely vast.

4. *Her.* And of what nature? Must it not be, Asclepius, of just the contrary? And is not contrary to body bodiless?

*Asc.* Agreed.

*Her.* Space, then, is bodiless. But bodiless must either be some godlike thing or God [Himself]. And by "some godlike thing" I mean no more the generable but the ingenerable.

5. If, then, space be some godlike thing, it is substantial; but if 'tis God [Himself], it transcends substance. But it is to be thought of otherwise [than God], and in this way.

God is first "thinkable" for us, not for Himself, for that the thing that's thought doth fall beneath the thinker's sense. God then cannot be "thinkable" unto Himself, in that He's thought of by Himself as being nothing else than what He thinks. But He is "something else" for us, and so He's thought of by us.

6. If space is, therefore, to be thought, [it should] not, [then, be thought as] God, but space. If God is also to be thought, [He should] not [be conceived] as space, but energy that can contain [all space].

Further, all that is moved is moved not in the moved but in the stable. And that which moves [another] is of course stationary, for 'tis impossible that it should move with it.

*Asc.* How is it, then, that things down here, Thrice-greatest one, are moved *with* those that are [already] moved? For thou hast said the errant spheres were moved by the inerrant one.

*Her.* This is not, O Asclepius, a moving *with*, but one *against;* they are not moved *with* one another, but one *against* the other. It is this contrariety which turneth the resistance of their motion into rest. For that resistance is the rest of motion.

7. Hence, too, the errant spheres, being

moved contrarily to the inerrant one, are moved by one another by mutual contrariety, [and also] by the stable one through contrariety itself.  And this can otherwise not be.

The Bears up there, which neither set nor rise, think'st thou they rest or move?

*Asc.*  They move, Thrice-greatest one.

*Her.*  And what their motion, my Asclepius?

*Asc.*  Motion that turns for ever round the same.

*Her.*  But revolution—motion round same —is fixed by rest.  For "round-the-same" doth stop "beyond-same."  "Beyond-same" then, being stopped, if it be steadied in "round-same"—the contrary stands firm, being rendered ever stable by its contrariety.

8.  Of this I'll give thee here on earth an instance, which the eye can see.  Regard the animals down here,—a man, for instance, swimming!  The water moves, yet the resistance of his hands and feet give him stability, so that he is not borne along with it, nor sunk thereby.

*Asc.*  Thou hast, Thrice-greatest one, adduced a most clear instance.

*Her.*  All motion, then, is caused in station and by station.

The motion, therefore, of the cosmos (and of every other hylic animal) will not be caused by things exterior to the cosmos, but

*Her.* 'Tis Mind and Reason *(Logos)*, whole out of whole, all self-embracing, free from all body, from all error free, unsensible to body and untouchable, self stayed in self, containing all, preserving those that are, whose rays, to use a likeness, are Good, Truth, Light beyond light, the Archetype of soul.

*Asc.* What, then, is God?

13. *Her.* Not any one of these is He; for He it is that causeth them to *be*, both all and each and every thing of all that are. Nor hath He left a thing beside that is-not; but they are all from things-that-are and not from things-that-are-not. For that the things-that-are-not have naturally no power of being anything, but rather have the nature of the inability-to-be. And, conversely, the things-that-are have not the nature of some time not-being.

14. *Asc.* What say'st thou ever, then, God is?

*Her.* God, therefore, is not Mind, but Cause that the Mind is; God is not Spirit, but Cause that Spirit is; God is not Light, but Cause that the Light is. Hence should one honour God with these two names [the Good and Father]—names which pertain to Him alone and no one else.

For no one of the other so-called gods, no one of men, or daimones, can be in any measure Good, but God alone; and *He* is Good alone and nothing else. The rest of things are separable all from the Good's nature; for all the rest are soul and body, which have no space that can contain the Good.

15.  For that as mighty is the Greatness of the Good as is the Being of all things that are —both bodies and things bodiless, things sensible and intelligible things.  Call not thou, therefore, aught else Good, for thou would'st impious be; nor anything at all at any time call God but Good alone, for so thou would'st again be impious.

16.  Though, then, the Good is spoken of by all, it is not understood by all, what thing it is.  Not only, then, is God not understood by all, but both unto the gods and some of men they out of ignorance do give the name of Good, though they can never either be or become Good for they are very different from God, while Good can never be distinguished from Him, for that God is the same as Good.

The rest of the immortal ones are natheless honoured with the name of God, and spoken of as gods; but God is Good not out of courtesy but out of nature.  For that God's nature and the Good is one; one is the kind of both, from which all other kinds [proceed].

The Good is He who gives all things and naught receives.  God, then, does give all things and receive naught.  God, then, is Good, and Good is God.

17.  The other name of God is Father, again because He is the that-which-maketh all.  The part of Father is to make.

Wherefore child-making is a very great and a most pious thing in life for them who think aright, and to leave life on earth without a child a very great misfortune and impiety; and he who hath no child is punished by the daimons after death.

And this the punishment: that the man's soul who hath no child, shall be condemned unto a body with neither man's nor woman's nature, a thing accurst beneath the sun.

Wherefore, Asclepius, let not your sympathies be with the man who hath no child, but rather pity his mishap, knowing what punishment abides for him.

Let all that has been said, then be to thee, Asclepius, an introduction to the gnosis of the nature of all things.

# Scientifica Hermetica

## An Introduction to the Gnosis of the Nature of All Things

### LESSON I

### The Nature of all Motion

1. *Hermes*. All that is moved, Asclepius, is it not moved *in* something and *by* something?

*Asclepius*. Assuredly.

*Her.* And must not that in which it's moved be greater than the moved?

*Asc.* It must.

*Her.* Mover, again, has greater power than moved?

*Asc.* It has, of course.

*Her.* The nature, furthermore, of that in which it's moved must be quite other from the nature of the moved?

*Asc.* It must completely.

We have here a discussion of motion. The three elements in all motion are the moved, the mover, and the vehicle or body in which this motion takes place. We are told that motion is through the principle of leverage, and that the elements of a lever are the Weight, the Fulcrum, the Power and the Lever. We must of course add to these four elements the Vehicle or medium in which the movement takes place. The thing to be moved is the weight, the Mover is the power, while the medium in which this motion takes place supplies the fulcrum and the lever. Any body that is to be moved must be moved within some field or space in which the motion takes place. This field or space in which the body is moved will have to be of much greater volume than the body to be moved, seeing that the movement is nothing other than the changing of the position of the moving body with reference to the space in which the movement takes place. Also, it follows that the mass of the space in which the movement takes place must be much less than that of the movable body. Given a body to be moved, and a space or vehicle in which this body is to move, the space or vehicle being far greater in volume and far less in mass than the body to be moved, we have then to find the nature of the mover, or that which is to cause the body to move in the vehicle. Mover must possess a greater degree of dynamic power than the thing to be moved, because we are not dealing with that which is absolutely static, but with bodies that have in themselves the capacity for a considerable degree of dynamic activity. This being the case, the mover, in order to move a body in a given direction must have the power to completely neutralize all of the tendency of the body to either stand still, or to move in a direction other than that in which the mover undertakes to move it. Given a mover therefore, having the power to overcome all of the power of the object to be moved, so that it is acted upon by the mover, which becomes the active and dynamic power moving the body, which is in relation to the mover, static and passive, we will have the body moved, provided there is the vehicle or space in which this movement is to take place but of course this space or vehicle must be composed of an altogether different order of substance to that going to compose either the mover or the thing to be moved. Thus the space or vehicle in which the thing to be moved must be ponderous and massive, while the mover must be of the active and dynamic nature. Thus we will have the three elements essential to the existence of motion. Without all three of these elements no movement is at all possible.

2. *Her.* Is not, again, this cosmos vast, [so vast] that than it there exists no body greater?

*Asc.* Assuredly.

*Her.* And massive, too, for it is crammed with multitudes of other mighty frames, nay rather all the other bodies that there are?

*Asc.* It is.

*Her.* And yet the cosmos is a body?

*Asc.* It is a body.

*Her.* And one that's moved?

3. *Asc.* Assuredly.

*Her.* Of what size, then, must be the space in which it's moved; and of kind [must be] the nature [of that space]? Must it not be far vaster [than the cosmos], in order that it may be able to find room for its continued course, so that the moved may not be cramped for want of room and lose its motion?

*Asc.* Something, Thrice-greatest one, it needs must be, immensely vast.

The kosmos is a vast body the most vast of all bodies. This being the case it is the greatest in volume of all bodies. As all the heavenly bodies and in fact all the solid bodies in existence are contained within the kosmos, it follows that it is a very massive body, seeing that in it are contained all of the solid bodies and hence all of the organized matter in existence. Notwithstanding this fact, the kosmos in itself is one body. It is a single body in which is contained all of the bodies in existence, but they are in it as parts of this synthetic or composite body, and yet it moves as one body. The kosmos, therefore, moves not only as a series of bodies, but as one single body. This kosmos, being in fact a single body, and being moved as a single body, and yet containing in itself all the organic matter in existence, must of necessity be of tremendous size, and yet, as it moves, it must move in space, and the space in which it is moved must be of so much greater extent that it will easily permit of all the movements of the kosmos within its space and still have space to spare. This necessitates the vastness of space.

4. *Her.* And of what nature? Must it not be, Asclepius, of just the contrary? And is not contrary to body bodiless?

*Asc.* Agreed.

*Her.* Space, then, is bodiless. But bodiless must either be some godlike thing or God

[Himself]. And by "some godlike thing" I mean no more the generable but the ingenerable.

Space must not only be of such immense volume that there will be within it ample room for all the possible movements of the kosmos, but it must also be of such a nature as to permit the greatest facility for such movements. Now, in as much as the nature of the Kosmos is to remain stationary, that is so far as moving as one body is concerned, it having to be moved by a mover apart from itself, and as this condition is due to the fact that it is a body, it can only move within a space which is bodieless. This is due to the fact that one body of matter can never pass through another material body of the same degree of density, hence there can be no movement unless there is a space in which the body is to move, that space being destitute of any bodies. Therefore, there must be in space no other bodies at all save the kosmos, which therefore moves in bodieless space. This space being in the very nature of things, bodieless, it must be one of two things, either it must be God, that is the Divine Essence; or else it must be something of a material nature and yet approaching very closely to the godlike nature. If of the latter nature, it will have to be above the plane of generation. The generable is that which ever tends to assume form, for generation is nothing other than the production of form, and hence, that which is generable must assume bodies; but the bodieless may never assume bodies, and hence is not subject to generation, therefore it must ever be the ingenerable. Space being the ingenerable, it must be that formless realm that abides above and beyond the range of the formal realm. Space must therefore be that formless state of substance which is ever diffused, and ever interpenetrates the Kosmos in all of its component bodies, in which each of its bodies floats, and in which each of them is suspended by attraction, and at the same time it must extend beyond the utmost boundaries of the entire kosmos, being in fact the expanse in which the whole Kosmos floats in which all the kosmic motions take place. It must therefore be one substance, in which there is no generative action and in which there exists no differentiation whatsoever. In such a vehicle alone could kosmic motion be possible. This is true because in this one medium must the kosmos move as a whole, and also in this space must all of the parts and bodies of the kosmos move with reference to each other and with reference to the whole kosmos. In this way are we able to grasp some conception both of the extension and of the nature and constitution of space as the field or vehicle in which all movement takes place, and without this ingenerable space, there could be no movement of the Kosmos.

## LESSON II

### The Nature of Space

5. If, then, space be some godlike thing, it is substantial; but if 'tis God [Himself], it transcends substance. But it is to be thought of otherwise [than God], and in this way.

God is first "thinkable" for us, not for Himself, for that the thing that's thought doth fall beneath the thinker's sense. God then cannot be "thinkable" unto Himself, in that He's thought of by Himself as being nothing else than what He thinks. But He is "something else" for us, and so He's thought of by us.

The difference between God and the godlike is in this: that the godlike is substance, but God Himself is Pure Essence. Space is substantial and not an essence, and therefore it cannot be classed as God but as the godlike. Essence transcends substance in that substance is the first form which Essence assumes.

In the process of thought, the thing that is thought, must fall beneath the sense of the Thinker. The sense spoken of here is rather equivalent to the Intelligent Principle itself. Thought being the product of this principle, must of necessity be the effect upon the Intelligent Principle of something acting as a suggestion, something stimulating it to activity. Thus we think of things as they impress the Intelligence. We think of them, not as they are in themselves, but rather as they present themselves to the Intelligence.  We can think of God, as something distinct from ourselves, and thus, He acts upon our Intelligence in such a way as to awaken corresponding thoughts about Him. For this reason we must at all times think of Him as something other than we ourselves.  Although the God-conception which every one has is in reality the creation of the man's own Intelligence, at the same time he must ever think of God as being something other than what he thinks of Him; that is, God must ever be thought of as a Divine Object of which we are striving to form an Intelligent conception, hence, He is ever in our thought, something Objective.  Therefore, while we are perfectly aware of the fact that our conception of God has been created by our Intelligence, yet we are unable to conceive of Him as being purely an Ideal Conception; we can only think of Him as something in Himself, apart from all that may be thought of Him.  Because of the fact that to our thought He is ever the one Absolute Reality, which man strives to understand, and yet can never know as It is in Itself, is God the Great and Supreme Mystery for our thought. But, just as we can never think of God as being anything but Real and distinct from our thought of Him: He can only think of Himself as being identical with what He thinks.  This is due to the fact that the very being of God in Its absolute sense is in His Thought.  God is nothing other but a Thinking Principle and the sequence of thought in which that Thinking Principle perpetually abides.  God, being Absolute Thought, can never conceive of Himself as being anything other than that Thought.  He lives in His Thought, in that He ever abides, and for this reason, to Himself, he is nothing other than what He thinks.  To us, this is inconveivable, for the simple reason that we can think only of something, hence we can never conceive of thought without something to be thought of, but God thinks only the Pure Thought, independent of anything to be thought of. The only subject of which He can think, is His own thought. Now, we cannot think of Space as thought, we can only think of it as space, as extension, and hence it is not thought of as thought, hence we cannot think of it as God, but as space, as some godlike thing therefore; but not as God Himself. Therefore, God cannot think of Himself, He merely thinks in the Absolute, but never thinks of Himself. Hence is He not thinkable to Himself.

6. If space is, therefore, to be thought, [it should] not, [then, be thought as] God, but space. If God is also to be thought, [He should] not [be conceived] as space, but energy that can contain [all space].

Further, all that is moved is moved not in the moved but in the stable. And that which moves [another] is of course stationary, for 'tis impossible that it should move with it.

*Asc.* How is it, then, that things down here, Thrice-greatest one, are moved *with* those that are [already] moved? For thou hast said the errant spheres were moved by the inerrant one.

*Her.* This is not, O Asclepius, a moving *with*, but one *against*; they are not moved *with* one another, but one *against* the other. It is this contrariety which turneth the resistence of their motion into rest. For that re-sistence is the rest of motion.

If space is, therefore, to be thought, [it should] not, [then] be thought as God, but space. If God is also to be thought, [He should] not [be conceived] as space, but energy that can contain [all space].

Space must never be confounded with God. Space is substantial, while God must not be conceived in this wise, but as energy, transcending space and containing within itself all space as it does all substance. It is this Divine Energy which contains the substance of space, and which permeates it through and through. In this way will one at all times be able to keep his thinking clear on the matter of God and Space; for space is the substance in which all bodies move, while God is the Divine Energy engendering all these motions through space. This Divine Energy is therefore more voluminous than space seeing that it contains all space.

Further, all that is moved is moved not in the moved but in the stable. And that which moves [another] is of course stationary, for 'tis impossible that it should move with it.

A body cannot move in another moving field, that is, the field through which the motion takes place will have to be stationary with reference to the body that is to be moved. The kosmos moving as a body, that is, as one body, and moving as such a body through space, it follows that space itself will have to remain absolutely stationary, and not merely relatively so. Also, the mover must be stationary with reference to that which it is going to move. That which moves the kosmos will have to be stationary with reference to the kosmos that is to be moved, hence the kosmos is in the position of that which is to be moved, that is it is the weight that is lifted or moved. Space is the medium through which, and in which the movement of the kosmos takes place. But the mover must be something else which is neither a part of the kosmos nor a part of space, but something distinct from both. It must be something which does not move, and which is not in space. It must be quite distinct from both. That which moves a thing cannot move with it, and likewise that which causes a motion must be distinct from the substance through which the object moves.

*Asc.* How is it, then, that things down here, Thrice-greatest one, are moved *with* those that are [already] moved? For thou hast said the errant spheres were moved by the inerrant one.

*Her.* This is not, O Asclepius, a moving *with*, but one *against;* they are not moved *with* one another, but one *against* the other. It is this contrariety which turneth the resistence of their motion into rest. For that resistence is the rest of motion.

The motion of the spheres is caused by the motion of one sphere against the other. While the Kosmos moves as a unit, also each of the spheres within that Kosmos moves with reference to the other spheres. This motion is not one of gravitation, for as a matter of fact there is no such thing as the attraction of gravitation. That which is taken for gravitation is in reality nothing else but the centrifugal force exercised by each of the spheres, which centrifugal force ever tends to repel all of the other spheres from it. It is this contrariety of repulsive force, the force emanating from one sphere neutralizing that of another, that turns this mutual resistance of motion into rest. The rest of motion is merely the result of this resistance of one centrifugal force by another. Thus we have through this mutual resistance of the repulsive forces of the diverse spheres the cause of the state of rest or passivity which is present in the intervening spaces between the realms of the diverse spheres, for every sphere is surrounded by a neutral area that isolates it from all the other spheres, and thus is preserved the stability of all the spheres in kosmos. There is no such thing as either gravitation or the principle of inertia in the sense that science speaks of them. Such nonsense belongs to the intellectual vacuity of the schools of learning, and of all science when divorced from the Hidden Wisdom.

7. Hence, too, the errant spheres, being moved contrarily to the inerrant one, are moved by one another by mutual contrariety, [and also] by the stable one through contrariety itself. And this can otherwise not be.

The Bears up there, which neither set nor rise, think'st thou they rest or move?

*Asc.* They move, Thrice-greatest one.

*Her.* And what their motion, my Asclepius?

*Asc.* Motion that turns for ever round the same.

*Her.* But revolution—motion round same —is fixed by rest. For "round-the-same" doth stop "beyond-same." "Beyond-same," then, being stopped, if it be steadied in "round-same"—the contrary stands firm, being rendered ever stable by its contrariety.

The fixed stars, through their repulsive force, drive the moving stars away from them until the latter are met with another repulsive force that turns them back and in this way, being caught between the two repulsive forces, they are forced to move in their respective orbits. It is the force of the fixed stars driving the moving stars away from them and also by the contrary force of the other moving stars that causes the direction of movement of the moving stars, and this is also what determines the orbits of all the moving spheres. There is no such thing as an orbit eternally fixed in time and space. As a matter of fact the orbits are continually changing and this could not be otherwise seeing that the orbit is fixed by the contrariety of the diverse moving spheres. As they are all of them continually moving and hence changing their relative positions the point where one contrary force will neutralize another will be continually shifting, and therefore, the orbits will be continually shifting from one position in space to another. It is in this way that although the positions of the orbits are continually shifting they are yet relatively the same distance apart, and preserve their mutual relations.

At the same time it is to be borne in mind that there are constellations which do not revolve around any fixed stars, but which move around their own centers of gravity as the term is commonly used. In the strictest sense of the word, all the spheres move around their own centers of gravity or to speak more accurately, around their own centers of repulsion as it is in reality the repulsive force that causes all motion. This is true because of the fact that gravity is merely an effect of repulsion. That which turns round-the-same, is merely that which turns round its own center of gravity, or more properly its center of repulsion, and this is determined by that which prevents it from going beyond this point and in that way describing a wider circuit. The contrariety of motion tends to neutralize all contrariety and all centrifugal force, and in this way to transmute motion into rest, and it is this neutral point, or place of rest, that determined the path of the constellation and therefore the extent of is orbit. All stability in the kosmos is therefore the result of the neutralizing effect of the contrariety of the diverse repulsive or centrifugal forces in the kosmos. It is this which preserves the relationship of the diverse spheres, and hence constitutes the stability and the integrity of the kosmos in all of its diverse parts. The synthetic unity of the kosmos is therefore absolutely dependent upon the contrariety of the diverse repulsive forces of the kosmos, and the state of rest which is brought about by this contrariety of the repulsive forces themselves. It is the law of contrariety therefore, on which the entire life of the kosmos is founded. This is the foundation of the universe, and there is to it no other fundamental principle of stability and motion.

## LESSON III

### The Mover

8.  Of this I'll give thee here on earth an instance, which the eye can see.  Regard the animals down here,—a man, for instance, swimming!  The water moves, yet the resistence of his hands and feet give him stability, so that he is not borne along with it, nor sunk thereby.

*Asc.*  Thou hast, Thrice-greatest one, adduced a most clear instance.

*Her.*  All motion, then, is caused in station and by station.

The motion, therefore, of the kosmos (and of every other hylic animal) will not be caused by things exterior to the kosmos, but by things interior [outward] to the exterior; such [things] as soul, or spirit, or some other thing incorporeal.

'Tis not its body that doth move the living thing in it; nay, not even the whole [body of the universe a lesser] body e'en though there be no life in it.

This principle of motion is very nicely illustrated by a man swimming.  The water moves, but the man, by the motions of his hands and feet is able to overcome the effect of this motion in the water, so that so far as he is concerned it is rendered motionless.  This result is realized by

reason of the fact that he imparts to the water
another kind of motion, counteracting the proper
motion of the water unto the end of its becoming
relatively motionless. It has become stable,
through the resistance which one form of motion
offers to another form of motion. Thus the water
is rendered stable so long as the two motions are
of equal strength, but if the motion engendered by
the hands and feet of the man should become of
a strength in excess of that engendered by the natural motion of the water he will, in that event,
be able to move through the water in opposition to
the natural movement of the water. Through the
contrariety of motion and the resistance engendered thereby, is one able to maintain himself in
the water and to move at will through it. In fact
the motion engendered by the man has rendered
the flowing water static in relation to the moving
body of the man. All motion must be causes in
station and by station, that is, the force that
causes a body to move must be stationary in reference to the body that is moved by it, and likewise
must the substance through which the body moves
be stationary in reference to the body that is moving through it, though in themselves both the
mover and that through which the motion takes
place may be in motion, but stationary in relation
to the moving body they must be.

The motion of the kosmos will not be caused by
something exterior to the kosmos, seeing that the
kosmos moves not en mass, but rather in all of its
parts severally, therefore, that force which acts
as the mover of the kosmos must move it in the
diversity of its separate parts, and not simply as
one great mass. This being the case, it follows
that that force which moves the kosmos, must per-

meate the entire kosmos in such a way as to act directly upon each separate portion of it. Hence, this motive force must not be something outside of the kosmos, but rather something vibrating through each of its separate parts, hence interior to the exterior of the separate spheres. In other words, the mover must reside within each part of the kosmos, and must move it through direct action upon its separate parts. At the same time, in order that this movement of the kosmic spheres may cause the kosmos to move as a unit, that is synthetically, it is essential that the force that is to move these kosmic spheres must be one force and not several forces. It must therefore be an undifferentiated and incorporeal force like soul, or spirit, or at least some force, devoid of the element of corporeality. This incorporeal force which we might very properly term the Anima Mundi or soul of the world, which is of necessity an universally diffused force and not a number of things, constitutes the real mover, which acting upon the spheres moves them through the substance of space. Each and every living material organism, is moved in this way, through the presence, within itself of this incorporeal force or spirit as the mover. Thus, they move not, because of an urge from without, but rather because of the urge which comes from within, and which is no part of the material organism, but rather something independent and yet residing within the organism. Thus do organisms move.

'Tis not its body that doth move the living thing in it; nay, not even the whole [body of the universe a lesser] body e'en though there be no life in it.

It is a mistake to assume that bodies move of themselves. There is no such thing as bodily motion. The body is not able to move itself, much less to move something else. A living body cannot even move a lifeless body. All motion is the result of the action of the mover operating through the instrumentality of the body. The body is merely the lever that is made use of by the mover for the movement of the weight that is to be moved. Not only is this true of ordinary living bodies, but it is also true that the whole body of the universe is unable to move in the slightest degree the very smallest body. This is true because of the fact that all organized matter moves in a mechanical manner. and hence it must have a force apart from itself to cause it to move. This being true, we must have the mover, as something distinct from the thing that is to be moved. The three elements must at all times be present, otherwise, no motion can possibly take place. There must be the mover, the thing to be moved, and the element through which the body moves. The whole body of the universe is the body to be moved, and space is the element through which it moves, therefore, the force that moves the body of the universe must be distinct from the universe and also from space, thus the mover is always another factor in the movement. Therefore, movement never originates in organic matter, but is in every instance something that results from the action of the mover upon the thing to be moved, and at the same time, this mover must act through space and be ever present and ever active in all portions of space. Were this not the case, the universe would never be moved. It is wrong therefore, for any one to assume that it is the united action of the universe upon its separate parts that causes those separate parts to move. No amount of physical matter can move the slightest particle of physical matter, seeing that all physical matter is in the category of that which is to be moved, and partakes not in the slightest degree of the attributes of the mover. From this it is seen that the entire theory of gravitation is wrong. Bodies do not, as bodies, have the slightest effect upon other bodies. The phenomenon of gravitation is not due to the mass of the body in the direction of which the smaller body is gravitating, but to the action of the mover upon this smaller body, and this mover can never be a physical organism, it must be something of a spiritual nature altogether.

9. *Asc.* What meanest thou by this, Thrice-greatest one? Is it not bodies, then, that move the stock and stone and all the other things inanimate?

*Her.* By no means, O Asclepius. The something-in-the-body, the that-which-moves the thing inanimate, this surely's not a body, for that it moves the two of them—both body of the lifter and the lifted? So that a thing that's lifeless will not move a lifeless thing. That which doth move [another thing] is animate, in that it is the mover.

Thou seest, then, how heavy laden is the soul, for it alone doth lift two bodies. That things, moreover, are moved *in* something as well as moved by something is clear.

As stated above, bodies do not move anything, they are merely the levers that are made use of to lift the things that are to be lifted. It is the thing within the body, the mover, which as we have previously shown is something incorporeal that is the mover, that causes the lifting of everything that is to be lifted, and this incorporeal mover must exert the force essential to move the body as well as to lift the weight. This will at once become clear if we try to understand the modus opperandi of a man lifting a weight. Take as an illustration, the moving of a weight such as one moves by the mere bending of the arm. This is caused merely by the contraction of the muscles, which in their contraction become shorter, and as the arm remains straight only so long as the muscles are relaxed, the contraction and therefore the shortening of the muscles, causes the arm to bend at the elbow, seeing that the arm cannot remain straight so long as the muscles are shortened in this way. The shortening of the muscles therefore, causes the arm to bend, and in this way, the weight is elevated by the application of a principle of leverage. It is the shortening of the length of the muscle, due to muscular contraction that causes the bending of the arm and the consequent lifting of the weight, and all other forms of lifting when performed by man are on exactly the same basis, that is, the contraction and hence the shortening of the muscles, this being the case, if we can find the force that causes this contraction of the muscles, we will have found out what it is that in reality lifts the weight. If one will examine a muscle he will find that it is made up of a great number of muscular fibres, and that each of these fibres is in reality a bundle of smaller fibres. When the most minute fibre has been examined it will be found to be composed of a number of Cells joined together, thus giving it its length. The contraction of a muscle begins therefore in these cells becoming crowded together, and in this way in the shortening of all of the fibres composing this bundle of fibre constituting the muscle. What is it that causes this contraction which is merely the crowding of the muscular cells together, and the relaxation of the muscle, which is equivalent to the separation of these cells again? There is but one possible explanation. There is a magnetic force that flows through the muscular fibre at all times. This force is charging each of these cells at all times. This force is subject to two motions, a centripetal motion which causes it to react upon itself, and in this way to bring the cells into close contact with each other, and also a centrifugal movement which causes it to flow out from itself as it were, and in this way to relieve the cells of this pressure and therefore to bring them into a state of loose contact. It is in reality this magnetic force under the dual aspect of the centrifugal and the centripetal movement, which acting upon the cells in this dual manner causes the contraction and the relaxation of the muscles upon which, first the lifting of anything depends, and secondly, the ability to put it down after it has once been lifted. Were it not for the relaxation of the muscles, they would always remain contracted, and hence it would be impossible for one to ever straighten the arm after it had once been flexed. Seeing that all muscular movement is absolutely dependent upon this dual activity of the magnetic force in its action upon the muscular cells, while flowing through the muscular fibre, the question that presents itself to our consideration is this: what causes this magnetic force to assume a centrifugal motion at one time and a centripetal motion at another time? It is not due to any law of periodicity because if that were the case we would only be able to lift anything at certain times, but as a matter of fact we can use our muscles at any time that we desire to do so. We are able to keep the muscles contracted until we are ready to relax them, and then at once they become relaxed and the weight is deposited at exactly the time that we wish to do so. This indicates the nature of the control that directs the mode of motion of the magnetic force. It is clear that it is our Desire that directs the motion of the magnetic force. How can desire control the mode of motion of a force? There is but one way that this could be possible, and that is on the assumption that Desire is itself a Force, and that this Desire Force is in continual contact with the magnetic force, and hence is at all times acting upon the magnetic force which responds to its action. The cause then of all motion is that the Astral Will Force is directly acting upon the Magnetic Active Force, and by causing it to act centrifugally or centripetally according to the desire of the Astral Will Force, the muscles are used as levers to bring about the desired result. The desire to lift any object is at all times a state subsequent to the thought that it should be lifted, and therefore, it is the mind that directs the action of the Astral Will Force. This being the case it follows that it is the action of Thought as a Fluidic Force, coming in contact with the Astral Will Force and through this causing the magnetic force to act in such a way as to cause the muscles to contract and relax in such a manner as to express in an active form the realization of the thought. This being the case, it follows that it is mind that acts as the mover, and that mind must move first the Will Force, then the magnetic energy, next the muscles, and then the whole body of the man, and last of all the weight that is to be lifted. It is the mind that is the mover, all the other factors are merely factors in the system of leverage that has to be employed in this lifting of the object to be lifted. It is then, not the body, but the soul that lifts everything that is lifted, and it is also the soul that puts them down. If this be the case, how are we to account for the fact that in many instances, one is unable to lift that which he starts out to lift, or after having lifted it, has to drop it before the time at which he desired to deposit it? In other words, what is the basis of muscular strength, and what constitutes muscular weakness? The strength of a muscle depends upon its degree of contraction, and upon the length of time during which this degree of contraction can be maintained. The effect of the weight is to overcome this contraction and to force the cells of the muscular fibre into the state of loose contact. Therefore the real contest is between the strength of the centrifugal motion of the magnetism circulating through the muscular cells, and the weight of the object to be lifted, and the consequent tendency to overcome this centrifugal magnetic action. Muscular strength then will consist first, of the number of muscular fibres, second, of the number of cells in each fibre, third, upon their degree of response to the action of the magnetic force; fourth, upon the quantity of that magnetic force; fifth, upon its response to the action of the Astral Will Force; sixth, upon the strength of this Will Force; seventh, upon the response of this Will Force to the action of Thought, and eighth, upon the strength and intensity of the power of thought. On these eight conditions depends all thought manifesting as strength, and hence upon them is dependent all strength. Physical strength is therefore, nothing but soul strength acting through a suitable system of leverage. This goes to show that the soul is the mover. As that which is below is equal to that which is above, it follows that it is the soul in everything that moves it, and that moves whatever appears to be moved by it. Soul is therefore the mover, while at all times bodies are the moved, though they are also the levers which the soul uses in order to move other things. All actions, even the most physical and material are nevertheless the actions of the soul. It is the one and only mover of all things that are ever moved. See, therefore, that thou shalt never confound mover with moved, for this would be very irrational. All things are done and all works are performed by the soul, bodies are but the soul is the one and only workman.

## LESSON IV

### The Bodiless

10. *Asc.* Yea, O Thrice-greatest one, things moved must needs be moved in something void.

*Her.* Thou sayest well, O [my] Asclepius! For naught of things that are is void. Alone the "is-not" is void [and] stranger to subsistence. For that which is subsistent can never change to void.

*Asc.* Are there, then, O Thrice-greatest one, no such things as an empty cask, for instance, and an empty jar, a cup and vat, and other things like unto them?

*Her.* Alack, Asclepius, for thy far-wandering from the truth! Think'st thou that things most full and most replete are void?

11. *Asc.* How meanest thou, Thrice-greatest one?

*Her.* Is not air a body?

*Asc.* It is.

*Her.* And doth this body not pervade all things, and so, pervading fill them? And "body"; doth body not consist from blending of the "four"? Full, then, of air are all thou callest void, and if of air, then of the "four."

Further, of this the converse follows, that

all thou callest full are void—of air; for that they have their space filled out with other bodies, and, therefore, are not able to receive the air therein. These, then, which thou dost say are void, they should be hollow named, not void; for they not only are, but they are full of air and spirit.

There is nothing void. All that is is filled with something, and only that which "is not" can truly be said to be void. This means that the void is only another name for "nothing." The point to be borne in mind is that no thing can be void. if there is a void, it is because there is nothing. all things must contain something. There can never be such a thing as a receptacle for nothing, therefore nothing can ever be said to be void of contents. Not only is this true of the existent but it is likewise true of the subsistent. Nothing is ever empty of contents. Were it empty it would not be. There is no such thing as an empty cask, an empty jar, an empty cup, or an empty vat. There are no vacuums. These things are not empty but hollow. All hollow things are filled with air. Air is a body composed of the same elements as are all other bodies. All bodies are composed of the union of the four elements: Earth, or the "cold" principle; Air, or the "dry element"; Fire, or the "hot element," and Water, or the "moist element." It is the union of these four elements that causes all the physical elements. All bodies are formed in this way, and it is the preponderance of the particular element that determines whether the body shall be of an Earthy, a Fiery, a Watery or an Airy nature. Whatever is composed of these four elements in diverse proportions is a body. Air in the atmospheric sense is a body, because it contains all of these elements in its composition, though because of the fact that the Dry element or Air is in the preponderance, it is of the nature of air. Thus it is to be seen that because air is made up of the blending of the "four" it is therefore a body as much so as is any physical organism a body. Hollow things being filled with air, they are filled with a body, and hence are full, and not empty.

That which is empty of fluids or solids is full of air, and that which is full of liquids or solids is empty of air, therefore, one thing is as empty as another, just as it is as full as another thing. To be filled with one thing means to be empty of everything else. We may exhaust the air in a hollow vessel but that does not make it empty, because though the atmospheric air is exhausted, yet are the four primal elements still there, and there is no way by which they may be driven from it, hence it is still full of the four primal elements, thus it is still full and not empty. As long as air, the "four" or even the spirit is present in any thing, it is not void but full of that which it contains. Therefore, there is, and can never be any such thing as a void in all the universe. All things are full, and we have nowhere a void but everywhere a Pleroma.

12. *Asc.* Thy argument *(logos)*, Thrice-greatest one, is not to be gainsaid, air is a body. Further, it is this body which doth pervade all things, and so, pervading, fill them. What are we then, to call that space in which the all doth move?

*Her.*   The Bodiless, Asclepius.

*Asc.*   What, then, is Bodiless?

*Her.*   'Tis Mind and Reason *(Logos)*, whole out of whole, all self-embracing, free from all body, from all error free, unsensible to body and untouchable, self stayed in self, containing all, preserving those that are, whose rays, to use a likeness, are Good, Truth, Light beyond light, the Archetype of soul.

*Asc.*   What, then, is God?

All things, that is, all material organisms, are filled with air being, in fact, nothing other than receptacles for air.   This is true because all physical organisms are more or less porous and the openings between the particles are filled with air. Above all things, however, the primal air fills all things.   The all is here used with reference to the entire Kosmos, not only the Kosmos perceptible by the senses but also the intelligible Kosmos as well.   This entire Kosmos moves as a single body though of course there are multitudes of bodies moving within it.   However, we have here to deal with the Kosmos moving as a single body.   Moving as a body it must move in something; that is, there must be a space in which the Kosmic Body moves, and that space must be something other than the Kosmos.   This space must be Bodiless for the reason that all bodies, as well as the All Body moves in it, hence it cannot be a body but must be just the reverse of body; that is, it must of necessity be bodiless.   Being bodiless it cannot contain the "four" but must be composed of something higher than the "four."   What can be the nature of this bodieless space which is not composed of the "four?" It is composed of Mind and Reason. Mind is the higher or Spiritual Principle, while Reason is the Manifestation of this Mind in Hyle. Mind and Logos then are the two Principles entering into the composition of Pure Space. These are not compounded of other principles but are in themselves Pure Principles. That is to say, they are Essences and not compounds, as are all other things. Mind and Reason are self-embracing or containing self within themselves. They are contained by nothing but themselves. They, in themselves, are one, there being nothing of their Essence contained in anything but themselves. This Bodieless Space exists nowhere but in itself. It is never transformed into anything else but is at all times this Pure Space and nothing else. It is free from all body for the reason that it can never assume bodily form, for the moment that it assumed bodily form it would cease to be itself. This is the Arupa or Formless realm. Here there can be no error for it is free from the misleading influence of form, and likewise it is composed of Mind and Reason alone. Hence it is all Intelligent. It can never be influenced by any body but it controls all bodies. It can never be taught by anybody, seeing that it is a different element from those going to compose all bodies. It is by reason of its own power and essence ever contained within itself and not in anything but itself. It contains all, for it is the space in which all moves. At the same time it must be understood that this Space is the Vehicle or Receptacle in which all that emanates from the Realm above it is deposited and preserved. Nothing can emanate from the Above which does not enter this Space and there abide. This is therefore the Vase or Element in which all the Rays are deposited and in which they are all preserved. These rays that enter Space and are there preserved are Good, Truth, Light beyond light and the Archetype of soul. The Good can be contained only in Space. It can originate only in the Realm beyond Space but it can be contained only by Space. When it acts upon Kosmos it ceases to be Good and straightway becomes Bad. Space is therefore the Reservoir of Good and the only place where it can manifest itself. This is also the reservoir of Truth which can originate only in the realm above Space but which manifests in Space. When it enters the Kosmos it becomes error seeing that Truth can never manifest through form. Light is merely the manifestation of the Spiritual Light, the Light beyond the light. Manas or the Mind Stuff of the Mental Plane is but the manifestation of this Spiritual Light. The White Light of the Mystic is nothing other than that Divine Light that manifests as the Mind of Nature and the Intellect of man, and in a still lower form as the Kosmic Light, the Light of the Sun being one of its lowest manifestations. This White Light can only act through Bodieless Space, when it contacts the Bodies it becomes something lower. This light is mirrored in Space and there preserves its identity to a certain extent. Though we must never make the mistake of assuming that this Light is Space, or that Space is this Light. Space is the Vehicle which is used by the Light, and the same is true of the Good and Truth. These rays of Good, Truth and the Light beyond light, are reflected in Space and are contained there as they can never enter bodies. It is the Space in which they move the same as it is the space in which

Bodies move, but the two Zones are distinct. There is the Rupa Zone in which all bodies move, and there is the Arupa Zone in which the Rays of Good, Truth and Light beyond light move. The twain never meet.

What is meant by the Archetype of soul? There is first of all the Absolute Life Ray which is transformed into Jiva the pure Kosmic Life Principle. This in turn becomes the Soul Essence, which is organized into individual souls, that is the soul of man. Its lowest manifestation is Prana or the Life Principle of the Universe, the realm of Zeus. We may symbolize these four rays by the rays of colored light. The Absolute Violet Ray is the Ray of Truth. In the highest sense the Indigo Ray, that is the Absolute Indigo Ray is the Ray of Good. The Absolute Yellow Ray is the Ray of Light beyond the light. The Absolute Orange Ray is the Ray of Absolute Life, while as Jiva it becomes the Absolute Blue Ray. As Soul Force it becomes the Absolute Green Ray, and as Prana it is the Red Ray. Of course this is merely a symbolic way of reaching an analogous understanding of the subject. This ray which is the Archetype of Soul, the Pure Life Ray is also reflected in Space, and with the other three rays it operates in space. These four Rays constitute the Mover which acting through Space, that in which all things are moved, causes the body of the Kosmos to move in Space. Thus we have the three elements or factors of all motion, the Four Rays of Good, Truth, Light beyond light and Life as the Archetype of soul, as the combined Mover; Bodieless Space as the field in which all movement takes place, and Kosmos as the Moved. God is yet something beyond all of these, great as they are. It is a mistake to say that God Himself moves anything or does anything. God is Transcendent, while the Mover is merely Transcendental. We must go back of the three factors of motion to find God. He is not this, but other, in His Pure Esse.

## LESSON V

### The Divine Essence

13. *Her.* Not any one of these is He; for He it is that causeth them to *be*, both all and each and every thing of all that are. Nor hath He left a thing beside that is-not; for they are all from things-that-are and not from things-that-are-not. For that the things-that-are-not have naturally no power of being anything, but rather have the nature of the inability-to-be. And, conversely, the things-that-are have not the nature of some time not-being.

God is not any of the things mentioned in the previous lesson, rather is He that which causes these things to be. Neither the rays of Good, Truth, Light beyond Light or Archetypal soul are in themselves self-existent. Their being is derived from God. Not that God creates them; but rather that they are the perpetual manifestations of His Beness. Not only is this true of those Supernal Rays, but it is also true of all the things that are. As all things emanate from Him, and are the manifestations of His Esse, there is nothing left that is-not. In other words, there can never be any such thing as a direct creation of something which was non-existent previous to such creation. In the absolute sense, all things are eternal in duration. Although, they may not at the given moment be in a state of existence in Space, they must be subsistent in God. Those things, subsistent in

God are being perpetually reflected in the Arupa realm of Space, and from this they are continually reproducing themselves in Kosmos. All things are therefore in God, and from Him are being made manifest in space. Hence, there is never a single new thing ever comes into being, but on the contrary, the norms are continually assuming formal manifestation, hence there is never any possible thing that is not at all times existent or subsistent. All things are from things-that-are, and never at any time from things-that-are-not. That is to say, nothing can ever come into being, unless it already is in God as a norm. A thing-that-is-not has absolutely no power to ever come into being, its only attribute is to remain non-existent. In other words, there is absolutely no power in the non-existent or rather non-subsistent to ever bring it into being. Also, God has no power by which He can ever bring the non-subsistent into being. He can only manifest Himself, and therefore, unless a thing is an integral part of His Being, He can never manifest it. In other words, God can only manifest that which is unmanifestly present in Him. Things-that-are-not, or the non-existent have no power of ever being and likewise, things-that-are, or the existent, have no power to ever at any time cease to be. In other words, that-which-is, can never become extinct. This is due to the fact that everything existent is but the manifestation of God, or rather of a correspondent in God, and hence no thing can ever be extinguished without first extinguishing its Archetype in God, hence nothing can ever be extinguished without first changing the nature and character of God. The Kosmos being the manifestation of God, it must be as unchangeable as God Himself. And also, God has not the power

to destroy anything at all, for seeing that it subsists in God, otherwise it would not exist in the
Universe, it follows that to destroy anything, He
would have to destroy a part of Himself. Therefore, all things are eternal, they always have been
and always will be. They are as endless as is God
Himself. Of course this does not mean that they
may never lose their material form. Their existence is in no sense dependent upon material form.
This is but an appearance. The form or so-called
entity is not the thing. The thing is the type, or
the species so to speak, and that type is eternal,
seeing that it is the perpetual manifestation of the
Archetype. The norm ever continues, and manifests itself at all times through ever changing
forms of expression, but the norm remains ever
the same. The Ideal Form is ever the same, but
the corporeal form is ever changing, but ever preserving the essence of the norm, and also of the
Ideal Form. Therefore, nothing is ever made in
the sense in which this term is commonly used.
That-which-is, ever seeks to be made manifest, and
the manifesting of the hidden that-which-is, is
what is erroneously termed the making of the
thing. All is in God, and is manifested from Him
into Kosmos through Space.

14. *Asc.* What say'st thou ever, then, God
is?

*Her.* God, therefore, is not Mind, but Cause
that the Mind is; God is not Spirit, but Cause
that Spirit is; God is not Light, but Cause that
the Light is. Hence should one honor God
with these two names [the Good and Father]
—names which pertain to Him alone and no
one else.

For no one of the other so-called gods, no one of men, nor daimones, can be in any measure Good, but God alone; and *He* is Good alone and nothing else. The rest of things are separable all from the Good's nature; for [all the rest] are soul and body, which have no space that can contain the Good.

God is not Mind, but Cause that the Mind is. Even the Divine Mind is not the Absolute God, rather is it that Divine Thought is spontaneously generated within God. God is an Esse one of Whose actions is to Think, and it is the perpetual sequence of this spontaneously generated Thought which constitutes the Divine Mind. God lives through His Thought, and hence Thought is one of the Essences of the Divine Esse. Mind is the livingness of this Thought, and is His Being though not His Beness. God is not Spirit, but cause that the Spirit is. It is wrong to say that the Absolute God is Spirit. Spirit is rather the Breath of God. It is a synonym for the Active Will of God, and is therefore, more in the nature of a ray from the God Center. We might even speak of Spirit as a mode of motion of the Divine Essence. Spirit is the Energy of God, but God is the reality back of that Energy. In the Bible Jesus is charged with the statement that God is a Spirit. This can of course have no reference to the Absolute God, but must relate to one of the lesser Gods. The One Spirit is not God the One, much less is it true to speak of Him as a Spirit. God is the Fount from which all Energy proceeds, and the Spirit is merely that First Energy that emanates from that fount. This is the true position of the Holy Ghost of Christian Theology.

There is still another mis-statement in the Bible, viz.: God is Light. God is not Light, but Cause that the Light is. The Light, in its highest sense is one of the Rays emanating from the Divine Center. He manifests through this Light. When Mystics speak of God as the White Light they demonstrate that they have absolutely no conception of the true nature of God. The White Light is nothing other than the synthesis of the seven colored rays of light, and these are all manifestations of that Absolute Light which emanates from God, but is not God. Buddhists do not worship this Absolute God, for the highest conception of the Mahayana Buddhists is Amitabha, or Boundless Light. Their Amitabha is therefore merely the purest aspect of the Light, while Bodhi or Enlightenmnt is the active expression of that Light. All of these are but manifestations of that Cultus of the light, which is only one of the Powers emanating from the One God. Therefore we must see in God the Fount of Mind, Spirit and Light; hence, Truth, Light and Spirit are Attributes of God, but not God Himself. They are the avenues through which His Being is expressed but are not in any sense of the word His Beness. We are therefore able to see the correctness of the Mystical Theology of Meister Eckhart, when he taught the Divine Darkness as being superior to the Light. He was initiated into the true nature of God, and is the only Christian Theologian of which the writer has any knowledge, who had reached this realization. His theology is far superior to that attributed to either Jesus, Paul, John or James. In other words, his teaching is Hermetic through and through. The Divine Darkness is the source of the Light. The Old Testament teaches this also. We are told that He dwelleth in the Darkness, that clouds and thick Darkness are round about Him. Wouldst thou find God? Then penetrate the Light until thou hast passed through it, and hast reached the point where there is no Light, but absolute and utter Darkness and thou wilt have found God. It is this Darkness that is the source of all. Just as all Magic Power comes from the Night Side of Nature, so does all the Divine Power come originally from the Night Side of Divinity or from the Divine Darkness. It is here that we find the greatest force. Just as in the heart of every flame of fire, there is a black flame that gives forth the heat to the white flame, so is it true that it is the Darkness of God that gives forth the Divine Light. It was this mystery that Eckhart had mastered and this was the Still Mystery of his teaching. Out of the Darkness cometh the Light. There wilt thou find the source of all. It is this mystery which is meant by the Initiation of the Black Veil. There are but two names that properly pertain to God alone, those of the Good and Father. We term Him the Father because all things are engendered by His Thought, and the Good or Ku because from Her are all things born forth. The Good is the same as the Motherhood of God. These are functions performed by God alone. All things are engendered by the Divine Thought, and are developed and brought forth into manifestation by the Divine Goodness or Ku. Hence to call Him the Good and Father is equivalent to calling Him the Mother and the Father.

The Good pertains to God alone. We cannot attribute It to any of the gods, to the daimones nor to man. It belongs to God alone. All other things are separable from the Good's nature. The reason for this is that they are all composed of soul and body, and soul and body have no place or space that can contain the Good's nature or the Good. This will at once appear when we realize that all bodies are made up of the blending of the four elements. Being composed of the four elements, it follows that no body can contain the Good, being filled with the four elements, there being no room for anything not composed of these four elements. Neither can soul contain the Good, seeing that soul is made up of that which emanates from the Divine Life or Energy. Soul force is the first mutation of Spirit, and as this soul force is what all souls are composed of, the soul being composed of soul force, it cannot contain Spirit, much less the Good from which Spirit emanates. There is no space in soul through which the Good can move, and hence the Good can never enter into the soul. Now the daimones can never contain the Good because they are Kosmic in their nature and are devoid of soul. Men can never contain the Good because they are composed of soul and body, and as such are incapable of containing the Good, seeing that It can enter neither soul or body. The Great Supernal Gods cannot contain the Good, because they are composed of the Soul Force, and as the Good can never contact soul directly, they are separated from the Good, offering no space for IT. The lesser gods can never contain the Good, seeing that they are devoid of Spiritual Soul, and hence there is no one of them all, containing any space through which the Good can manifest itself. Hence Good can be only in God alone, and He is Good alone.

## LESSON VI

## The Essence of the Good

15.   For that as mighty is the Greatness of the Good as is the Being of all things that are —both bodies and things bodiless, things sensible and intelligible things.  Call not thou, therefore, aught else Good, for thou would'st impious be; nor anything at any time call God but Good alone, for so thou would'st again be impious.

The might of the Greatness of the Good is as the Being of all things that are, whether they be things bodieless, or bodies, things sensible or intelligible beings.  The Pleroma of all things, all bodies, and all bodieless things, all things perceptible by the senses and all things comprehensible by the intelligence, ever subsists in the Good. The Intelligible Kosmos, or the Ideal World has been born from the Good, and is perpetually maintained by the Good, hence it subsists in the Good, though existing in Space.  The Universe of the Kosmos perceptible by the senses, has in reality been projected from the depths of the Good, hence it subsists in the Good, though existing in space. All bodies are engendered in the depths of the Good, and hence subsist in the Good, though existing in the Kosmos.  The Bodieless or Arupa realm is engendered in the depths of the Good, and therefore subsists in the Good, though existing from It.  This being the case, the norm of all is perpetually present in the Good, and a thing exists, solely because of the fact that its Archetype subsists in the Good. The Being of everything is therefore inherent in the Good, and hence there is nothing which can possible have any existence if separated from the Good. As all things exist not of themselves, but due to the fact that they subsist in the Good, it would be a grave impiety were we to attribute Goodness to anything else save God, or to call anything God save the Good alone. This is true because that which is the fundament, the origin and the ultimate cause of all must of necessity be God the One. The relation which God must bear to all things is born by the Good, and therefore, there can be no place for God seeing that the Good is exactly what God would have to be; therefore, in order that God may be, He must be synonymous with the Good, therefore God and the Good are identical. They are not two, but one, the Good is God and God is the Good.

16.    Though, then, the Good is spoken of by all, it is not understood by all, what thing it is. Not only, then, is God not understood by all, but both unto the gods and some of men they out of ignorance do give the name of Good, though they can never either be or become Good. For they are very different from God, while Good can never be distinguished from Him, for that God is the same as Good.

The rest of the immortal ones are natheless honored with the name of God, and spoken of as gods; but God is Good not out of courtesy but out of nature. For that God's nature and the Good is one; one is the kind of both, from which all other kinds [proceed].

The Good is He who gives all things and naught receives. God, then, doth give all things and receive naught. God, then, is Good, and Good is God.

It is out of ignorance that some men give the name of Good to the gods and to men. It is wrong to speak of anything save the One God as being Good. Neither men nor the gods can ever be or become Good. To become Good, either a man or a god, must completely lose his nature, and ceasing to be either a man or a god, must become the Good, that is, he must become Ku. As there can never be but the one Ku, it will follow that all individualization will be lost and that it will mean that the man or the god must completely lose his identity in Ku, being completely absorbed in Ku. Goodness is not a moral attribute that can be manifested by a man or a god, or anything of things that are; it is the absolute Essence of Ku. It can never be confined in anything at all. There is a difference between God and the gods or men, and it is this very difference that renders them what they are instead of being God. When they were born out of God, it was the impartion of this very difference that caused them to come into their present life as something other than God. This same difference that distinguishes them from God, distinguishes them from Good, for there can never be any distinction between God and the Good. Good being merely the Essence of God, it follows that all things, existing as they do in their distinction from God, exist in their distinction from the Good. The Good is the nature of God, and whatever nature anything else may have, that nature distinguishes it from the nature of God, that is from the Good. In order that they may become Good, they will therefore have to lose their own nature, and acquire the nature of the Good, and that would mean that they had attained the nature of God, and if they have the nature of God, then of necessity they are God, and as this God must be One, it follows that they will cease to exist the moment they become Good. That is why Jesus refused to be called Good, he knew that there can be but the one Good One, and that the Good can never enter the world of form, hence were the Good to incarnate in form, it would at once become Bad, seeing that the Good can never be contained in any form either of body or soul. The Good then is inseparable from God, and all other things, being in their nature different from God are therefore different from Good, hence they are not-Good. The Good is therefore an Ideal which must ever be held before man, but like the pots of gold at the end of the rainbow, it is an Ideal which he can never reach, because were he to reach it he would be no longer a man, or even a god, but the One God. This would be his Maha-Para-Nirvana, which would be his final and complete extinction as a person and his absolute absorption into the Divine Esse. As Good is the absolute nature of God, any one in order to be Good, must be absolutely of that nature and essence, hence he must be Very God of Very God of one substance with the Father, and in fact he will have to be the Father absolutely. Hence we can see the distinction between God or the Good and all things else. Although the Good has given birth to all things, yet the very act of giving birth to them, was the act of depriving them of all Good. She cannot bring forth anything Good, for to bring forth is to squeeze out of it all the Good. All becoming is through the deprivation of Good. Therefore, is it true that all existence is through Evil as distinguished from Good.

The rest of the immortal ones are honored with the name of God and are called gods out of courtesy to their immortal nature. Because they do not perish as do things having bodies, they are somewhat similar to God, hence we call them gods. However, they are not Good. God is Good not out of courtesy but because the Good is His nature. They are one and have the same kind. All other kinds, that is all Genera and Species of what ever order they may be, either mortal or immortal, in fact everything save God, proceeds from this nature of God which is Good. It is the source of all other natures. As all natures are derived from the Good which is the nature of God, they are not Good. The Good can only be attributed to that nature which is self-contained and self-sustained, and is in no sense dependent upon anything else.

**The Good is He who gives all things and naught receives. God, then, doth give all things and receive naught. God, then, is Good, and Good is God.**

The Good must be that which gives all things and receives nothing in return. A Good deed must be performed without any thought of reward. As long as one looks for reward for a deed, he is of necessity doing it for the sake of a reward, and hence is actuated solely by his own personal interest. At least this factor must be taken into consideration. The very essence of Goodness, if we view it from the ethical standpoint, is disinterested benevolence. There can be no such thing as

Goodness in the transaction unless this element of disinterestedness is present, and this disinterestednes must be absolute, there must not be the slightest element of self-interest involved, if there is, it will be a selfish act and not an unselfish one, hence it cannot be Good. It is utterly impossible for any man to ever do a disinterested deed. He may wish to do it but it is utterly impossible for him to do it. This is true for the simple reason that it is quite impossible for him to ever do a deed of a beneficent nature toward another, without at the same time benefitting himself. All of our so-called good deeds benefit us more than they do anyone else. An evil deed will injure the one who perpetuates it more than it will anyone else. This being the case, to do good and refrain from doing evil, is merely the most effective way to promote one's own interests. The Law of Compensation is such that one can never fail to reap a reward for all of his good deeds and to suffer the penalty for all of his evil deeds. This being true, it is impossible for anyone to do a good deed which is not the best possible business policy on his part. In other words, every good deed is in the nature of an investment which always pays the highest possible dividends. It is a gilt-edged security in fact. For one to lead the Spiritual Life, is utter selfishness. This is true because by so doing one is merely promoting the growth of his own soul, hence he is insuring his own best interests. The Spiritual Life is not a life of service to God, but a life of service to the one who is living it. It is merely the course by which one may secure his own best interests. There is nothing unselfish in the ascetic life. The purpose of the ascetic life is to secure control over the appetites and instincts, and to bring the body into subjection to the will, is it not absolutely to the interest of any one to have control over the passions and desires, to be master of his instincts? It is merely intelligent selfishness that causes anyone to lead the life that will insure the realization of what he has in his mind as the most desirable thing. The fact that must ever be borne in mind is that one can never do the right thing at any moment without conferring a benefit upon himself which he could not possibly have conferred in any other way. This being the case, there is no such thing as unselfishness in any human action, we are merely looking out for number one all the time. Religions have at all times instinctively recognized this law and have made use of it. They have taught that God would reward the righteous and punish the wicked, and in this way they have pointed out the self interest in doing right. Some religions have of course urged unselfishness, but they have at the same time held out the bait for the righteous and have held out the warning to the wicked. The Philosophical Orientals have not taught so much the idea of rewards and punishments as they have the Law of Karma, this same Law of Compensation mentioned above. In this way they have all stimulated the self-interestedness of their followers to do right. At first it may be urged that there is a vast difference between the heavens promised by the different religions, but if one will look at the matter seriously he will soon see that they all alike appeal to human selfishness, but that the promise is changed in different religions so as to present the most alluring possible bait to the particular class to which they appeal. The Mohammedan Paradise is a place where they will all be rich, will dress fine, will live in the height of luxury, and will have all the beautiful women that they wish; in other words, each True Believer will have the most glorious Harem and Palace that he can possibly conceive of. The Christian Heaven is to be paved with all manner of precious stones and gold, the gates are pearls, and there is wealth untold. No wonder the Americans and Europeans do not want to change their religion? No matter how poor we may be here, if we are Christians we will all be rich beyond the dream of avarice when we die and go to heaven. The Norse Viking had a religion that appealed to him very strongly. In Valhalla, you eat and drink until you can eat no longer, and cannot get any drunker, then you get up and fight, until most of you are killed and all are covered with wounds and can stand no longer, then you go to sleep, and when you wake from your refreshing nap, you are perfectly well, all the dead have come to life, and everyone is perfectly fit, having no headache and you are hungry and thirsty again, and so you start to feasting all over again. The Indian's heaven is the Happy Hunting Ground, where there is always an abundance of game, no fatigue and no white men. The Hindoo Svarga is a realm of sensuous delight. Now it is easy enough to see that all that one does in order to reach any one of these heavens will be utter selfishness; but how about the Buddhist Nirvana, a conception which many Hindoos also hold to? It is just as selfish as the others. While the others appeal to the lusts of the body, Nirvana appeals to the lust of the soul. To the one who hungers and thirsts for the spiritual life, no heaven will be at all attractive to him unless it offers him an opportunity to gratify his spiritual longings. Reincarnation appeals to human selfishness, for it teaches that the good man will be happy in his next incarnation, and the bad man will suffer for his misdeeds. Thus all appeal must be an appeal to selfishness. This is perfectly right, for it is the law of life that a righteous life will promote our highest good.

There are others who teach that one should be unselfish, and that he should do all his good deeds without thought of reward. These are more intelligently selfish than any of the others! For the less of selfish thought one devotes to a good deed, the greater merit will it carry with it, and hence the greater benefit will he derive from it! Therefore the most selfish thing in the world is unselfishness! As we can do absolutely nothing without reaping a reward, all of our deeds are performed in our own interest, seeing that no one benefits so much from the deed as the one who performs it. But that is not all. We not only do not give anything without reaping a greater benefit, but we are able to give absolutely nothing which we have not previously received. God gives everything that is, and hence we receive everything from Him, we merely pass it along when we need that which the giving of it will bring, worse than we do the thing that we give. Hence we give nothing. We relinquish the less that we may secure the greater good. God gives all things, hence no one else gives anything. God can receive naught, because everything that is, is perpetually present in Him, therefore, He can receive nothing seeing that all things are already in His possession. Because He can receive naught, seeing that it is already His, and because everything that is has come from Him, hence he is the giver of all things, and as it is the nature of the Good to give all and receive naught, it follows that God is Good, and Good is God. This is a situation which applies to God alone.

This nature of God was clearly recognized by Meister Eckhart, and so he formulated the idea of Disinterested Love for God as the only truly religious life. He said that one should love God while being absolutely indifferent to the love of God. He should devote all to God asking nothing in return. This Holy Indifference at first is a rather seductive dogma; but will it hold water? Suppose for argument's sake, one was able to actually live this life? If he loved God and asked for nothing in return, if there was such a thing as a man loving and serving God without an axe to grind, would not such disinterested love on his part awaken the love of God for him as nothing else would do? If so, he would be securing a greater measure of God's love than he could possibly secure in any other way. In other words, this idea of disinterested love is merely an attempt to put one over on God, to place God under obligations to love you, while pretending that you are not particularly anxious about His love. Do you not know that there is nothing that will awaken gratitude so much as the belief that the one to whom you are grateful has no desire for your gratitude? To serve God and ask for nothing in return, is the most effective way to secure an abundant return, it is the most profitable investment that one could possibly make. This being the case, there is no such thing as disinterested service to God, seeing that the more disinterested it is, the more effectively are you promoting your own interest. To love and serve God is absolute selfishness.

But there is another aspect of the matter. It

is utterly impossible for anyone to serve God at all. Do you, perchance imagine for a moment that God is in need of your assistance? What benefit can you by any chance confer on God? What can you do for God? Is not He absolutely self-sufficient? Were you to pass out, would He know that anything had happened? The contemptible self conceit of anyone imagining that he can do anything for God is truly amazing. The only thing that could be classed as service to God, is to manifest as near as possible the Attributes of God in your own life. To manifest His attributes would be to promote the evolution of your own soul in the most effective manner possible, and this is of course to insure your greatest good, hence this manifestation in your own soul of the attributes of God will be, not serving God, but serving yourself in the most effective way conceivable. When men talk of serving God, they in reality mean to serve themselves! Is it serving God to lift up humanity? Certainly not, at most it is serving those particular human beings that you lift up in that way. But as we have previously shown, the Law of Compensation will bring to you the reward for such good deeds, and hence you will be serving yourself more than anyone else. Some imagine that by teaching the Truth, they are serving God, but the fact is that there is no way by which our faculties and attributes grow so much as by their exercise, and hence by teaching the Truth, we are merely enlarging our capacity to know the Truth, therefore, we are merely employing the most effective methods of searching for the Truth. This being the case, one is merely promoting his best interests. By expressing the highest in us, we are only giving it exercise! Why will you not be honest and frankly admit that

when you are working for the Spiritual Regenera-
tion of Society you are simply taking a little bit
of Spiritual Gymnastics and developing your
soul? The facts in the case are, man and everything else, receives all and gives nothing, while
God gives all and receives nothing, therefore is
God alone Good. Goodness is merely another
name for the nature of God.

What is stated with reference to man is also
true of all the gods and intermediary beings, none
of them are Good because none of them are unselfish. A disinterested deed can never be performed
by anyone who will by the performance of such
act be promoting his interest in the most effective
way possible. Selfishness is not a sin, it is the
Law of all Life save that of God alone. There is
no such thing as either Altruism or Piety, they
are both merely intelligent Egoism. Goodness is
the nature of God and of nothing else, therefore,
no one else may do Good, but must seek self-ex-
pression, for that is in reality the result of everything that they do. All that they do promotes
their own best interests, and hence they can in
the very nature of things do no disinterested act.
Religion is not disinterested, even the religion of
the Mystic or the Gnostic, it is in fact the strug-
gle of the soul for life. People mistake Spiritual
Self-seeking for disinterested devotion but it is
nothing of the kind. All is bad save God and He
is Good alone. Let not man deceive himself, he
has been trying to be God Almighty long enough,
let him try being a man awhile for a change. He
may succeed at that, but he is sure to fail in his
efforts to make himself God. One Absolute God
is quite enough at a time, but the more real men
we can have the better. If man would only be

content to be himself, instead of trying to be God Almighty, he would make a much better job of it. The two greatest injunctions ever given are that from the Temple of Isis, Man know thyself, and this one from me, Man be thyself. In these two injunctions are summed up all the wisdom of all the ages.

## LESSON VII

### The Nature of the Father

17.  The other name of God is Father, again because He is the that-which-maketh-all.  The part of father is to make.

Wherefore child-making is a very great and a most pious thing in life for them who think aright, and to leave life on earth without a child a very great misfortune and impiety; and he who hath no child is punished by the daimons after death.

And this the punishment: that the man's soul who hath no child, shall be condemned unto a body with neither man's nor woman's nature, a thing accurst beneath the sun.

Wherefore, Asclepius, let not your sympathies be with the man who hath no child, but rather pity his mishap, knowing what punishment abides for him.

Let all that has been said, then, be to thee, Asclepius, an introduction to the gnosis of the nature of all things.

In addition to the Good, God is called the Father, because He is the that-which-maketh all.  Because all things that are made are made by Him.  In the proper sense of the word He is both the Father and the Mother, seeing that it is the mother much more than the Father that maketh.  As the Archetypes of all things subsist in Ku, and are there prepared for birth into existence, it is true that they are all made in Ku and by Ku. Thus are they brought forth from subsistence into existence. Thus is God the maker of all things that are made, or that come into manifestation, and hence is He termed the Father, and we might say the Mother as well. This is because it is the function of the parent to make and hence is God the true and Absolute Parent. Physical parents are merely the instruments that are made use of by this Divine Parent in the manifestation of His work of making children.

Because of the fact that the making of all things is the function of God as the Father, child-making has been considered a very great and a most pious thing in life. It is impossible for man to imitate the Good seeing that this is quite impossible for anyone living an individualized life, but man can imitate the Paternal function of God. He can do the work of making physical bodies for children. This is the only Divine thing a man can do. For this reason it is a most pious thing to do, seeing that there is nothing so pious as the duplication of the work of God. It is even contended that it is a great impiety for anyone to leave this earth life without a child. To understand this doctrine we must take into consideration the Egyptian Doctrine of Reincarnation. It was held that it took several incarnations to produce a Gnostic; that in fact, Gnostics are born, they are not made. The belief was that no one could reach the Old Old Path unless he has during several incarnations been striving after the Gnosis of the Beautiful and the Good. Therefore, the only hope for the world was that the souls on the Path should be continually reincarnating on earth. Also it was held that the only way for anyone to reach the Gnosis of the Good was for the soul to be able to reincarnate several times after he had started to climb the Ladder of Life. Therefore, to deny him the opportunity of reincarnating was equivalent to refusing him the chance to attain the Gnosis of the Good. But they also held that a soul could only reincarnate through the instrumentality of parents who were close to his own plane of life. In other words, they would contend that it was out of the question for one who was devoted to the Religion of the Mind, to come into incarnation through the agency of impious or ignorant parents. He could only incarnate through a father and a mother, both of whom were wise and pious people. This will lead us to the conclusion that when a devotee of the Religion of the Mind shall pass out, he cannot again incarnate unless he can find a father and a mother each devoted to the Religion of the Mind. This being the case, the percentage of souls on the Path who may incarnate will be dependent upon the number of men and women devoted to Gnosis, who are willing to assume the duty of parenthood. Now, he would contend that there are never at any time as many Gnostic souls in incarnation as there are out of incarnation, and therefore, everyone of those who shall refuse to have children will to that extent be sentencing some Gnostic Soul to remain out of incarnation. Not only will they be doing an injury to that soul, but they will also be depriving the world of the blessing of having that Gnostic Soul living in it, which will be a great calamity. Thus we see the great importance of the paternal and the maternal function in the work of elevating the world. There is this aspect of the matter in addition to the duty of man to celebrate the mystery of the Divine Making of things. Not only is this true of the Great Souls however, it is also true of all other souls that as a rule, they seek parents of their own peculiar type and stage of unfoldment. In fact the inconsistences in the types of parents and children are largely due to the fact that the souls cannot find parents of their own type, or the husband and wife are not of the same type, or else it is for lust and not for child-making that they have the relation. Also, it is true that the normal use of the sex function for almost every one is the making of children, and hence, if one has not reached the point where the sex function can be made use of in the right manner spiritually to fail to use it for child-making is to decline to let it find expression at all. The contention here made is that for the man who does not use his sex force in child-making, the soul must reincarnate as an Hermaphrodite. This is due to the fact that not having used his sex energy, it will atrophy and as a result the daimons will cause him to incarnate in such a way as to render it impossible for him to perform this function. According to Hermes, all the people who are born without the true sex are such souls bearing the punishment alloted to them by the daimons.

The problem that is here presented is a rather difficult one of solution. It is doubtless true that the small number of superior souls incarnate at any one time is due to the fact that most superior souls prefer a life of chastity, and hence have no children. This means that there are never any great number of superior souls undertaking the parental function at a time, and therefore, only a comparatively few great Souls can incarnate in a single generation. This keeps the old souls and especially the Enlightened souls out of incarnation and only permits the young and ignorant souls to incarnate. Of course to a certain extent, this difficulty has been overcome by reason of the men and women, who through the exercise of their sex force on people already born are regenerating them so as to make them the twice born. It may as well be said that this is the only way that one having no child can discharge the obligation. They must either enable great souls to incarnate, or else they must regenerate the souls already here. One of the great needs of this generation is a training school where men and women will be trained and disciplined to fit them for the performance of the function of bringing great souls into incarnation. Fatherhood and Motherhood should be taken out of the haphazard category that they are in at the present time, and should be placed among the learned professions, and they should receive a Degree as Master of Fatherhood or Motherhood before they undertake to perform that work of Art. The other great work that is needed is a training school to train them for the work of Spiritual Fatherhood and Motherhood in order that they may perform the work of regenerating the souls already in incarnation. To a great extent however, the statement made in our sermon relates to the time at which it was given. At that time the evolution of the race was through man and woman. The evolution of the Cycle now dawning will be the development of the Androgyne type from which we came, and hence it is now a very great and a very pious work to evolve the double-sexed condition in oneself. This being the case we must not lay too much stress upon what he says here. While the Hermaphrodite was at that time a thing accurst beneath the sun, it is now a thing thrice blest.

This sermon is in the nature of an introduction to the gnosis of the nature of all things. The principles laid down in these seven lessons must ever be taken as the foundation of any study into the nature of things. This is of course only the introduction to the study, but only on these principles can anyone gain an insight into the rich mine of Hermetic Science. These principles must be taken at all times as the foundation of our investigations, and without these principles, it will be futile to try to understand the next three lessons. This science is the only real science. The so-called Exact Sciences are untrue in almost every respect. These are the true principles of the relation of all things.

# Scientifica Hermetica

## The Sacred Sermon of Hermes

### TEXT

Parthey (G.), *Hermetis Trismegisti Poemander* (Berlin, 1854), 31-33.

Patrizzi (F.), *Nova de Universis Philosophia* (Venice, 1593), 8b 9.

Mead (G. R. S.), *Thrice Greatest Hermes* (London, 1906, Corpus Hermeticum III (IV).

1. The Glory of all things is God, Godhead and Godly Nature. Source of the things that are is God, who is both Mind and Nature,—yea Matter, the Wisdom that reveals all things. Source [too] is Godhead,—yea Nature, Energy, Necessity, and End, and Making-new-again.

Darkness that knew no bounds was in Abyss, and Water [too] and subtle Breath intelligent; these were by Power of God in Chaos.

Then Holy Light arose; and there collected 'neath Dry Space from out Moist Essence Elements; and all the Gods do separate things out from fecund Nature.

2. All things being undefined and yet unwrought, the light things were assigned unto the height, the heavy ones had their founda-

tions laid down underneath the moist part of Dry Space, the universal things being bounded off by Fire and hanged in Breath to keep them up.

And Heaven was seen in seven circles; its Gods were visible in forms of stars with all their signs; while Nature had her members made articulate together with the Gods in her. And [Heaven's] periphery revolved in cyclic course, borne on by Breath of God.

3.   And every God by his own proper power brought forth what was appointed him. Thus there arose four-footed beasts, and creeping things, and those that in the water dwell, and things with wings, and every thing that beareth seed, and grass, and shoot of every flower, all having in themselves seed of again-becoming.

And they selected out the births of men for gnosis of the works of God and attestation of the energy of Nature; the multitude of men for lordship over all beneath the Heaven and gnosis of its blessings, that they might increase in increasing and multiply in multitude, and every soul enfleshed by revolution of the Cyclic Gods, for observation of the marvels of the Heaven and Heaven's Gods' revolution, and of the works of God and energy of Nature, for tokens of its blessings, for gnosis of the power of God, that they might know the fates that follow good and evil [deeds] and learn the cunning work of all good arts.

4. [Thus] there begins their living and their growing wise, according to the fate appointed by the revolution of the Cyclic Gods, and their deceasing for this end.

And there shall be memorials mighty of their handiworks upon the earth, leaving dim trace behind when cycles are renewed.

For every birth of flesh ensouled, and of the fruit of seed, and every handiwork, though it decay, shall of necessity renew itself, both by the renovation of the Gods and by the turning-round of Nature's rhythmic wheel.

For that whereas the Godhead is Nature's ever-making-new-again the kosmic mixture, Nature herself is also co-established in that Godhead.

## LESSON VIII

### God, Godhead and Godly Nature

1.  The Glory of all things is God, Godhead and Godly Nature.  Source of all things that are is God, who is both Mind and Nature,— yea Matter, the Wisdom that reveals all things. Source [too] is Godhead,—yea Nature, Energy, Necessity and End, and Making-new-again.

Darkness that knew no bounds was in Abyss, and Water [too] and subtle Breath intelligent; these were by Power of God in Chaos.

Then Holy Light arose; and there collected 'neath Dry Space from out Moist Essence Elements; and all the Gods do separate things out from fecund Nature.

The trinity here introduced is God, Godhead and Godly Nature.  It is rather difficult to differentiate between the three, owing to the fact that the definitions overlap.  This is due to the fact that one of these principles may be one thing in itself, and yet its manifestations are identical with what another is in itself.  For instance, the source of all things is God, who is Mind, Nature and Matter as well as the Wisdom that reveals all things, while at the same time Godhead is spoken of as Nature, Energy, Necessity and End and Making-new-again.  This will show that while Nature is the third aspect of the Trinity it is yet included in God and the Godhead each. This discrepancy will disappear however, when we realize that God is the Ultimate Mind working in Conjunction with Ku, and that this God manifests itself in action, and the synthesis of such manifestation is Nature and her manifestations, the Godhead being the Synthesis of the Powers that are emanated out from God, and that manifest themselves as Nature the Third Person of the Trinity. God is the Subject, Godhead is the Predicate and Nature is the Object, and yet they are one sequence. God is described as the Wisdom that reveals all things. Things are revealed when they are brought forth out of Ku, and have assumed an individual existence. The Wisdom that reveals them is the Thought which causes them to come forth into manifestation, the particularity of the Divine Thought. Thus God is the Creative Thought, the Maternal Essence and the Particularizing Thought which brings all things into outward manifestation. It is the thinking-manifest of God. All else, while in a certain sense it is God made manifest, it is not God in the Absolute, though emanating from Him. Godhead is the Unity of the Powers emanating from God. It is the coming to a head of all the Divine Emanations. The first of these Powers is the Divine Energy, the Life Energy and the Creative Energy that emanates from God. First appears this Pure Energy as the first Emanation from God. Next, there develops within this Energy as its First Differentiation, Necessity, or Fate. Before this differentiation takes place, Energy is Chaotic, having no direction whatsoever. After this differentiation, Energy has assumed a given direction from which it can never deviate. This is the Will or Fiat, called by the Arabs, Kismet; by Christians Predestination or Foreordination; by the Irish, Luck; by others, Destiny, Providence or Fate. It is that determining principle that is here termed Necessity. It is this which necessitates the course that all things must take. It is the Suchness of the Buddhists, that which makes all things such as they are. There can never be any direction for forces to take save that which grows naturally out of the direction of this Divine Necessity. All tendencies are started through Necessity. The Second Differentiation of Energy is the first differentiation of Necessity, and is the End. This simply means that Necessity has a goal in the direction of which it must move. This is the true meaning of Predestination. Each expression of Necessity must move in the direction of the realization of a definite end. In this sense, it may be said that that end is predestined through the operation of that particular expression of Necessity. In other words, each manifestation of Necessity must run a definite course, and at the end of this course, the predestined and necessary result must be brought about. The final differentiation of this Four-fold Godhead is Making-new-again. When the course of Necessity has reached its End, and has come into the accomplished realization of its course of development, this end which has been realized, does not remain stable, but on the contrary it is Dynamic, and hence, it becomes the Archetype or Norm of another course of Necessity, and so on unto infinity. Thus all that is in the entire course of Life and action is but the Sequence of Necessity, End and Making-new-again. Out of this manifestation of the Energy, Necessity, End and Making-new-again of the Godhead, Nature is but the natural sequence of the same process operating through the Kosmos.

Darkness that knew no bounds was in Abyss, and Water [too] and subtle Breath intelligent; these were by Power of God in Chaos.

Although the differentiation had entered into the Divine Energy, and these tendencies of Necessity, End and Making-new-again had entered into it, yet Order had as yet not been introduced. and as yet Energy was Chaotic in all of its Space. There were certain differentiation there, but they were also Chaotic. There was boundless Darkness, with not a ray of Light, for Light had not as yet been separated from the Darkness. At this time, Light was contained within the Darkness, and Darkness not having been polarized, there was no Light apart from the Darkness. All Light was Latent in Darkness. Old Night was supreme. Also, in this Abyss or the Great Deep was Water. The Heavenly Waters of Space. Throughout all Space was the Water, that is the Primordial Water or Moist Nature. This Water is the Truth of Water or the Great Mother Substance of Space. Also was there subtle Breath, the Truth of Breath, or the Masculine Dynamic Energy of Space. This was the Primal Air, or the Dry Nature. All these, Darkness, Water and Breath were by Power of God in Chaos, that is they were the Mutations through Nature of the corresponding Principles of the Divine Nature manifesting through the Godhead. In the Breath was latent the Intelligence that was to become Kosmic Thought.

Then Holy Light arose; and there collected 'neath Dry Space from out Moist Essence Elements; and all the Gods do separate things out from fecund Nature.

Darkness was polarized so that Holy Light arose from out of Darkness and shone forth in Space as being separate and distinct from the Darkness. From this we are able to see how absolutely scientific is the account of Creation given in the Book of Genesis. Let us look at the account given there and compare it with what we are told in our Sermon. In the beginning God created the heavens and the earth. And the earth was without form and void and Darkness was on the face of the Deep, and the Spirit of God moved on the face of the Waters, and God said ''Let there be Light'' and there was Light. In other words, the earth was Chaotic and empty, Darkness was on the face of the Abyss of Waters, and the Spirit or Breath moved upon the face of the Water, and Light appeared and we are further told that God separated the Light from the Darkness, that is, Darkness was polarized so that Light became a distinct principle in space. The rest of the first chapter of Genesis is in perfect accord with our Sermon. Light arose out of Darkness. Then Darkness is the source of Light. When God asks Job, ''Canst thou tell the place where Light dwelleth,'' the answer should have been, ''In impenetrable Darkness.'' This Darkness is the Night Side of Nature, the natural correspondent of the Divine Darkness. It is in this Darkness that all the Latent Powers of Nature abide. They are enchained in this Darkness. The purpose of Magic is to set free these forces of the Night Side of Nature and to make use of them. All science consists in the harnessing of these forces after they have been set free, and the work of Practical

Occultism deals with the freeing of these Night Side Forces. The initiation of the Black Veil consists of this very work and is the key to its performance. The Initiation of the White Veil on the other hand, relates to the mysteries of the Active Side of nature, and the use of forces already at liberty. The Black Art is the Art of setting Free the Latent Forces of the Night Side. From this it will at once be seen that Black Magic is much higher and more Divine than White Magic. Black Magic employs the Night Side Forces of Nature, and therefore, those forces not at present operative in Nature. On the other hand, White Magic only makes use of the Day Side Forces, and hence the forces of the Light. Therefore, White Magic is concerned with the Manifest Universe as it is, but Black Magic is that side which elevates the Universe itself, and for that reason tends to promote its higher evolution. This Darkness and Light are the Ahriman and Ahura Mazda of the Persians, and this shows that Arhiman is the higher God of the two. Black Magic is the true road for the acquisition of Supreme Power. The White Magician observes Natural Law, but the Black Magician is superior to Natural Laws, and is the Master of Nature not her servant as is the White Magician. For this reason, we have for ages discredited the practice of Black Magic as much as possible, and have made the Occultists believe that it was evil, and that it must be avoided. We have created for every religion a Satan, who is the God of Black Magic, so that he might act as a scarecrow to frighten our dupes away from the Night Side Forces, in order that we might have the power which the Holy Black Art would supply. While we have warned others against the practice of Black Magic, we have always practiced it ourselves. We would have continued in this course, and continued to exercise this power, for the people have no business with the Night Side Forces, were it not for the fact that for the past fifty years, many have refused to be fooled by our warnings, and have dabbled in the subject, and in this way have secured control of some of the Night Side Forces. As they have been bad people in the main they have used these Powers for evil purposes, and hence have endangered the stability of the Universe. It has therefore become our duty to place the Key in the hands of the better class in order that there may be a great many more who will understand the Key and will therefore be able to counteract the evil inuence of those dabblers in this Black Art. At the same time, we wish to warn our students against placing any credence in the Rituals of Black Magic. They have been prepared by us to fool the dabblers, so that they will either be frightened away from the Art, or else, if they practice it, following a lot of harmless mummery, they will acquire no power to speak of. Also, those Rituals are very dangerous, because they are so constructed as to bring the one who uses them into the power of the Hostiles on the Astral Plane, so that he will never reach the Night Side Forces. At the same time, it may be stated that the instruction for making the sacrifices, is perfectly correct, only this instruction is Esoteric, and its literal meaning will in every instance, throw you off the track. The real key to Black Magic will be given in subsequent lessons that will be issued by us; but remember, the formulae for Black Magic will only be given by a Master to his personal Disciple. We will never tell you how to do it, save at the Temple Door. At the same time, we tell you in these lessons, if you can read the Riddle which we propound to you, but remember you will have to read between the lines and catch us off our guard to find it.

When Holy Light arose from Darkness, it acted upon the Moist Essence, or Water, and by acting upon it in an attractive manner it caused the Elements, latent in the Water to come forth out of the Water, so that they became distinct Elements and were drawn forth from the Water. These Elements were collected beneath Dry Space, or Light. The meaning of this is that they were drawn forth into the Sphere of Light. Abiding there they become the primal Elements of the Manifestation. Thus was the first actual step in Manifestation taken. Now into this realm were the Gods projected, and they began the work of separating things out from Fecund Nature. Nature was now fecundated by Breath and Light, and the Gods acting upon Her, separated that which corresponded to each one of them, so that each provided for himself a sphere of manifestation, a vehicle through which he might express himself. Thus were the areas of spaces corresponding to the several Gods brought forth into existence. With the separation of things out from Fecund Nature by the Gods, we come to the end of the Divine Creation. All that follows after this is the work of the gods, and in no sense the work of God. God is the Maker of Nature, but the operations of Nature are committed to the several gods.

## LESSON IX

## The Birth of the Cyclic Gods

2.  All things being undefined and yet un-wrought, the light things were assigned unto the height, the heavy ones had their foundations laid down underneath the moist part of Dry Space, the universal things being bounded off by Fire and hanged in Breath to keep them up.

And heaven was seen in seven circles; its gods were visible in forms of stars with all their signs; while Nature had her members made articulate together with the Gods in her. And Heaven's periphery revolved in cyclic course, borne on by Breath of God.

At this stage in the creative process, we find that all things were undefined and as yet un-wrought. That is, the Elements were drawn forth into Dry Space or the Sphere of Light, and all things had been separated out from Fecund Nature, at the same time, things existed more as types than as anything else. They were not defined one from another, neither were they wrought into shape. It was more the spirit of the thing, than the thing itself that was in existence. All below the Elements was in a state of Chaos. At this time the light things, that is, those having the most intense rate of vibration, were drawn up into the height, in other words, they were drawn up into the region of the Divine Creation, and were directly suspended from it, so that they were the first strata, so to speak, suspended from the sphere of the Divine Creation, and became the first beginning of the Kosmos. The heavy things spoken of here are primeval or kosmic earth, that is, the earth principle in the kosmos, the earth spoken of in the first chapter of Genesis. When those heavy things were drawn forth and differentiated, they had their foundation laid down underneath the Moist part of Dry Space. Dry Space be it remembered is the Sphere of Light. The moist part of this would be the Heavenly Waters contained within the Sphere of the Light. The meaning of this statement is, that the heavy things, or primeval Kosmic Earth, were held in position by attraction on the part of the Waters within the Light Sphere, so that they were held in the sphere immediately below the sphere of these Waters, while the light things were suspended in the sphere above the Moist part of Dry Space. The universal things, are those of an abstract nature, that can never at any time enter into concrete form. They are in a sense the Types of Being, though not things in the material sense of the term. They are universal in contradistinction to the particular. They are what some would term the Laws of Nature, though in a sense they are the Logoi or Ideas that express themselves through actual manifestations. They are the Over-souls of all things, and are the patterns that all things must follow. They are the Norms in fact. These universal things, were bounded off by Fire, that is, the sphere of Fire separated them from the particular things. They were between the sphere of Heavenly Water and that of the Fire. This intervening space between the sphere of Water and that of Fire, is filled with Breath or the Primal Air. The universal things are suspended in this sphere of Air or Breath. The Water separates the universal things from the light things, and the Fire separates them from the sphere of particular things. Thus are they suspended in the sphere of Breath or Air. All such things are kept in their position by reason of the Breath which prevents them from coming into conjunction, the one with the other. They are held in this position because of their airy nature and the attraction which is exercised between them and the Breath. Thus was created the sphere of the Universals, and below this must abide the sphere of Particular Things, for it can never be that the two should ever meet. Thus was formed the lowest arc of the Æonian Realm and the Creation of the Æons. Kosmos must stretch from here into the Mundane region.

And Heaven was seen in seven circles; its Gods were visible in forms of stars with all their signs; while Nature had her members made articulate together with the Gods in her. And [Heaven's] periphery revolved in cyclic course, borne on by Breath of God.

The Fire is differentiated into the Seven Fires, or the Seven Gucumatz, the Serpents with dazzling Azure Wings. These are the Archetypes of all that is to come. They are the Rulers of Heaven. From each of the Seven Fires there starts a Circle of Force that passes through space and returns into its source. Thus is formed the Seven Circles of Heaven, and in each of these Heavenly Circles abides its peculiar choir of Daimones, thus is originated the seven choirs of Daimones. These seven circles constitute the seven zones of Heaven. Thus are the Great Hierarchies formed. Heaven's Gods were visible in forms of stars with all their signs. To understand this it must be borne in mind that the stars are not merely physical bodies, they are much more. There is the star, but resident within it, is the Subtle Principle of the Star, and still within this, is resident the God who rules it. The Star is therefore, little else than the Image or Statue ensouled by the God. When the Stars are spoken of as gods, it is not the star itself, but rather that which ensouls the star that is thought of. A Constellation, spoken of in a certain sense as a sign, is in reality the form or rather the group of forms, ensouled by an entire Hierarchy of the gods, demigods, daimones, genii heroes and spirits. The stars are the visible forms in which reside the gods which operate through them. The members of nature, are the diverse aspects of her manifestation. These members are made articulate with the gods in her, for the simple reason that all the active forces of Nature are nothing other than the operations of the Gods through them. There is no state of separateness between the Gods and the operations of nature, the forces of nature, respond at all times to the Gods that manifest through them. The phenomena of nature are nothing other than the appearances of the Gods through the vehicle of natural forces. There is no such thing as a Natural Law, what men in their ignorance term Natural Law is but the operations of the Gods resident in Nature. The periphery of Heaven was caused to revolve in cyclic course. The Heavenly Circles being caused to revolve, and in this way, cycles were produced, during each of which, the universe of matter, is under the dominance of a certain Hierarchy of the Divine Ones.

It is this revolution of the Heavenly Circles that causes all the Cycles that we pass through. What Theosophists call a Chain, is in reality the passing through one of these Circles of Heaven. These Chains or Circles have absolutely nothing to do with the Principles of nature, or even with the Planets, though they mistakenly think that they have. This is also the reason why there are only seven of these Chains in a World Period.

These revolutions of the Circles of Heaven are borne on by Breath of God, that is, the power that moves the revolutions of the Heaven is the Divine Breath, operating through the Fires that circulates through the Circles and in this way, acts as the motive power causing them to move as they do. This will indicate that the revolutions of the Heavenly Circles must at all times conform to the cyclic law operative in the Divine Breath. In other words, the life of the Breath of God is directly reflected in the cyclic revolutions of the Heavenly Circles. No one can ever understand Creative Evolution until he has mastered this Law of the Cyclic revolution of the Circles of the Heavens. It is the key to the evolution of the universe and of the human race. All the time during one of these Cycles, the world is ruled by the Hierarchy of that Cycle, and at the close of that Cycle, the Hierarchy must give way to the Hierarchy of the next succeeding Cycle. For this reason, there can never be a religion that is permanent in its forms. The religion for a definite period of time must conform to the Gods ruling during that particular Cycle. When a nation or a race comes into being, it comes into being under that particular Hierarchy that is ruling at the time of that Cycle, and that type persists through all subsequent Cycles, at least to a great extent. This is in reality the cause of the Cyclic Law that is seen to operate through all human history. Astrology will ever fail until Astrologers learn to make use of the Cycle in their computations. This is the true explanation of the Devils. During a Cycle, the evolution of the Universe must be regulated by the Gods of that Cycle, for this is the time when the Cycle must perform its work in the evolution of the universe. Therefore, evolution depends upon the absolute rule of the Gods of the Cycle. Now in case some other Gods exercise an influence at this times, they will be interfering with the work of the Gods of the Cycle, hence they will interfere with the Cyclic Gods themselves, therefore they will be Satans, or Adversaries, hence they will be Devils, though they are Gods in their own Cycles. In this law will be found the true key to the nature of the Hostiles. Nations rise and fall under the operation of this Cyclic Law. This is the reason why some nations and races are beloved of the Gods, while others are hated of them. This is why the Cyclic Gods are partial to some people and are the enemies of others. The Cyclic Revolutions of these Heavenly Circles is the Fate which even the Gods are subject to. This applies only to the Gods of Heaven. Those above Heaven, that is, the Great Supernal Gods, are not subject to the Rule of Fate or the Revolution of the Circles of the Heavens. This Law of Cyclic Change through the revolution of Heaven's Circles is the great Law that governs all actions, and that determines what is right and what is wrong at any given time. This is the Master's Secret, and He who knows this secret, is able to mount above all law and to be what he wills to be, for it is the key that unlocks the future. This is the real reason why Divine Incarnations must come to the earth from time to time, in order that a message for the time and age may be given to the world. It is for this reason that in the time of such a God-Man, the teachings of all previous God-Men cease to be authoritative, seeing they apply to other Cycles, while his message applies to the present Cycle. We are living now in such a period of change, and for that reason the teachings of all the past Masters fail at this time. The only safe guide now, is the instructions of the Dorado of this Cycle.

## LESSON X

### The Work of the Cyclic Gods

3.   And every God by his own proper power brought forth what was appointed him.  Thus there arose four-footed beasts, and creeping things, and those that in the water dwell, and things with wings, and everything that beareth seed, and grass, and shoot of every flower, all having in themselves seed of again-becoming.

And they selected out the births of men for gnosis of the works of God and attestation of the energy of Nature; the multitude of men for lordship over all beneath the Heaven and gnosis of its blessings, that they might increase in increasing and multiply in multitude, and every soul enfleshed by revolution of the Cyclic Gods, for observation of the marvels of the Heaven and Heaven's Gods' revolution, and of the works of God and energy of Nature, for tokens of its blessings, for gnosis of the power of God, that they might know the fates that follow good and evil [deeds] and learn the cunning work of all good arts.

The Kosmic Creation was not the work of God but of the gods.  After once Nature and the Gods in Her had been formed, the creative work of God, and of the Great Supernal Gods was finished, and henceforth, all creative work that was to transpire in Nature, must be the work of the Gods in her. Each of these Gods, has his own nature, just as definite as that of any other being. He could only manifest that nature in his creative action. These Gods created things by making manifest their own energies and their character. Every God created by his own proper power, that is it was the energy of each God that was the creative principle that brought into manifestation, those things which were latent within the essence of the God. By what was appointed to each God, we are to understand that which corresponded to the nature of that God. Thus the four-footed beasts, the creeping things, those dwelling in the water, the winged things, the seed-bearing plants, the grass and the flowers were all the work of different Gods. There was a God at the head of each of these Orders, and subject to him were a number of lesser Deities each of whom had charge of one of the Genera of that Order. We are not to understand that this was on the earth. Rather was this creation or birth in Heaven. It was later that they all took form in the earth life. We find this in perfect accord with Genesis, where it is stated that God created every beast before it was upon the earth, and every plant before it grew. These were the types that were afterward to manifest in earth life. This doctrine does not contradict Evolution. It only shows that Evolution can never produce an Order; it must work through the Orders created by the Gods. They will have to create another Order before Evolution can work along any other line than those already laid out for it. These things were created as types in the Heaven, and then in the course of time they assumed bodies on the earth. Each body assumed being in correspondence with the nature of the thing that was to live in it.

In them all were inherent the seed of again-becoming, or in other words, of reincarnation. This will appear at once, when we realize that they were of an Heavenly nature anterior to their physical existence. As they did not commence their existence as physical organisms, but as super-physical things, each of which later on assumed a physical form, as their vehicle of consciousness for the Physical Plane, it will follow that the loss of the physical form will not interfere with the higher life of the thing. They will therefore live out of the body until such time as they require another physical existence, when they will reincarnate. Seeing that their original existence on the earth was an incarnation, it is only natural that that which has pre-existed and has therefore come into one incarnation, should again incarnate as many times as it is essential for it to do so. Thus we have the commencing of the earth life of plants, animals, fishes, birds, reptiles and insects as well as grasses and flowers, each order starting on a course of Evolution through repeated incarnations, until such time as it has come to the end of its Karma, and has there become crystallized.

And they selected out the births of men for gnosis of the works of God and attestation of the energy of Nature; the multitude of men for lordship over all beneath the Heaven and gnosis of its blessings, that they might increase in increasing and multiply in multitude, and every soul enfleshed by revolution of the Cyclic Gods, for observation of the marvels of the Heaven and Heaven's Gods' revolution, and of the works of God and energy of Nature, for tokens of its blessings, for gnosis of the power of God, that they might know the fates that follow good and evil [deeds] and learn the cunning work of all good arts.

While it is not true that the Gods created man, that being the work of God, who created the Anthropos, who descended into Heaven and there became the Human Race; yet is it true that man by coming into the Heaven and separating into the race of men, became subject to the control of the Gods of Heaven. While man in his soul is the superior of the Cyclic Gods, nevertheless are his births or incarnations subject to the control of these same Cyclic Gods. The births of men, or their incarnations are regulated in accordance with the revolutions of the Cyclic Gods. In other words, there are men, corresponding to the nature of each of these Gods, and the work of each of the Gods having control of the births of men, is to bring into incarnation the particular men that correspond to His nature. It is wrong to say that anyone can incarnate at will, or that his Karma will bring him into incarnation at the time it is ready to do so. The incarnations of men are determied by the action of the Gods having control over the births of that particular type of man. The highest types of men are those selected for gnosis of the works of God and for attestation of the energy of Nature. These two types are the Scientists who are able to expound Nature, and the Philosophers who are able to understand the work of God. Such people do not belong to the ordinary human multitude, but are specially sent into incarnation by the Gods at such times as they are needed to aid in the evolution of the Race. They are caused to incarnate in the environment where they will secure the training best calculated to fit them for the work they will have to perform. The Gods do not inspire men, they simply send into incarnation the men who will naturally know the things that are to be done at the time. It is futile to try to educate men into Scientists and Philosophers; scientists and philosophers are born, they are not made. These men are all Men of Destiny, and they must perform the work for which they came into the world.

The multitude of mankind is made to incarnate for lordship over all beneath the Heaven, that is for the earth, and for gnosis of the blessings of Heaven. The mission of the average man is to subdue the earth and all that it contains, and to understand the blessings of Heaven, but not the work of the Realm above Heaven. The average man has no business knowing anything about God, or even the Great Supernal Gods, such knowledge is the heritage of Gentlemen, he is concerned with the earth and the Heaven, and has no business looking above his station. His other duty is to reproduce his kind. As it requires many work-men, but few thinkers, it is the duty of the Cheap Organisms to multiply as rapidly as possible in order that there may be many to do the work for which they are admirably fitted. All souls are en-fleshed by the revolution of the Cyclic Gods. Each of these Cyclic Gods has his own group of souls, and they can only come into incarnation at the time that the Cycle of their God is in operation. The humanity of a Cycle is at all times made up of the souls that properly belong to that Cycle.

All other souls have to wait until another time when their Cycle comes into manifestation. This explains why it is that each Cycle presents to us a given type of humanity, the souls corresponding to the God of the Cycle are incarnate, while the others are out of incarnation, and must wait until their turn comes.

Each Cyclic God brings into incarnation seven types of souls, though they all pertain to that Cycle. This is due to the fact that while a Cycle has a God over it, yet he has seven demi-gods under him, and each of these demi-gods caused the type of souls corresponding to him to come into incarnation during this Cycle. Thus, in every Cycle there will be found seven types of souls, and hence, seven types of men. These are what might be termed the seven casts of the race at the time of the Cycle. These have nothing to do with social classes, but are solely due to the type of soul to which they belong. The first type have as their life work, observation of the marvels of the Heaven and the revolution of the Gods of Heaven. The study of these things is the work of this type. They are what we might term the Occult Scientists. The second type have as their life work the study of the works of God and the energy of Nature. They are in a sense the Cast off Occult Philosophers, and should devote all of their time and energy to research of this kind. This is their mission in life. The third type are concerned with a study of the tokens of the blessings of Nature. They should study to discover the tokens that will indicate the blessings that Nature has in store for man. They are the Cast off Prophets and Prognosticators. This is their life work. The fourth type have as their work in life gnosis of the power of God. They are the Gnostics and Hermetic Wise Men whose duty it is to know the power of God, to preserve the Divine Mysteries, and to hand them on to posterity. The fifth type are those whose mission in life is to study and understand the fates that follow good and evil deeds. It is their work to let the people know what is moral and what is immoral, and to warn them of that life which leads to happiness and that which leads to pain. These are the ministers of religion and the teachers of Ethics. To do this work, one must know the workings of the fates that are operative in the particular Cycle in which they live, so that the morality they teach will be in accordance with Natural Law operative at the time. The sixth type are concerned with the cunning work of all good arts. They are the artists, the Craftsmen, the inventors, and their life work is to exercise their ability in those directions. The seventh type are the workers, whose mission in life is to labor with their hands under the direction of those placed over them. Their duty in life is to work. If they are faithful in this duty, they have accomplished their mission in life. Thus, every Cycle produces the types of soul that are essential to the work of that Cycle, so that its evolution may go on without interruption, and may come into its consummation for the next Cycle that is to take the place of the present one. In some instances, the humaninty of one Cycle is not suited to be the parents of the humanity of the next Cycle or is not suited to do the work of the one being ushered in, so much so that they would be in the way of the next Cycle. In this case, when the new Cycle is ushered in, the Cyclic Gods and their assistants, first destroy all the undesirables or at least the vast majority of them, so as to make room for the souls of the New Cycle. This is to a great extent the explanation of those natural disasters, pestilences, and wars that rage the country over at such times. The European War is such another means of clearing away the rubbish, in order that a new type may take the place of the present one. For that reason, the gods will see that it continues for some time yet, in order that its work of destruction may be complete, and the unfit may be removed, and may make room for the fit. History is never understood until we study it in the light of the revolution of the Cyclic Gods being the real power that rules the world. All theories are wrong. The one great determining force in life is the influence of the Cyclic Gods. What is wrong at one time may be right at another, and what is right at one time may be wrong at another. The only standard by which right can be measured is the work of the Cycle and the purpose of the Cyclic Gods. Whatever will promote their purposes is right, whatever will interfere with that is wrong. That is the one standard by which all things must be measured. The type of men that is most desirable at any given time is the type that will most thoroughly carry out the work of the gods of that particular Cycle. It is that which constitutes the Race Spirit at any given time. The Will of God as it is termed, which is supposed to rule the world, is in reality the energy of the Cyclic Gods of the particular Cycle in which the earth moves at the time.

4. [Thus] there begins their living and their growing wise, according to the fate appointed by the revolution of the Cyclic Gods, and their deceasing for this end.

And there shall be memorials mighty of their handiworks upon the earth, leaving dim trace behind when cycles are renewed.

For every birth of flesh ensouled, and of the fruit of seed, and every handiwork, though it decay, shall of necessity renew itself, both by the renovation of the Gods and by the turning-round of Nature's rhythmic wheel.

For that whereas the Godhead is Nature's ever-making-new-again the kosmic mixture, Nature herself is also co-established in that Godhead.

The life of man is regulated by the Cyclic Gods. His incarnate life is given him by them, and they also provide him the means of growing wise through the experience of this incarnate life, and in that way do they develop his consciousness and thus promote the evolution of the personality. This evolution of the men is regulated by the course of life which is provided for them through the revolution of the Cyclic Gods. In other words, this changing of cycles provides a change in the circumstances of life, most propitious for the evolution of every possible angle of personality. It is the revolution of the Cyclic Gods that regulates human fate. In order that man may be perfected so far as the universe goes, and in that way enter the realms above, he must pass through all the cycles, and in the majority of cases, through each of them several times. Death is also provided by the revolution of the Cyclic Gods, and it is a most important element in the evolution of a soul. Man evolves in exact proportion as his personality is transformed by the energy of the

Cyclic Gods.   He can evolve no more rapidly than his personality is transformed by them.   Life in the body will greatly depend upon the transformation of the physical body, for the interior principles can express themselves only so far as the body will give expression to their vibration.   Thus it appears that individual evolution will depend upon the man having a body that will respond to the vibration of the Interior Principles and to that of the energies of the Cyclic Gods.   When the time has come that it will no longer respond to them, all growth will cease.   The body, being formed of physical matter, it will not respond to this vibration with any thing like the rapidity that the higher principles will respond to it.   The result is that in the course of time, the higher principles will have so far outstripped the body in this response to vibration, that it will fail to keep in touch with them and as they can only express themselves through the body, their future evolution will be brought to a standstill.   Then the man dies.   After he has been dead for a time, the revolution of the Cyclic Gods will bring him into incarnation again.   At the time of his incarnation, the forces of such incarnation will cause the formation of a body exactly suited to his state of development at that time.   In other words, at the moment of birth, his interior principles and his body will be at the same stage of development. He will therefore progress for a time, until he has outgrown his body, when he will discard it, and through the revolution of the Cyclic Gods will procure another, so that he may pursue his age long evolution once more.   Death is therefore not a tragedy in any sense of the word, but on the contrary, it is an essential step in the evolution of consciousness.   In a word, it is one of the conditions of man's living and growing wise, and exists for this end. Without death, there would be no reincarnation, and without reincarnation there would be no change of bodies, and without the change of bodies there could be no perpetual progress through life. Therefore, look on death as a blessing, not as a misfortune.

**And there shall be memorials mighty of their handiworks upon the earth, leaving dim trace behind when cycles are renewed.**

During a given cycle there is developed a certain type of humanity, and this humanity develops a civilization, a culture and a religion of their own. This civiliziation, culture and religion are in every instance the expression of the type of that people. At the close of the cycle that produced it, this people disappear from the earth. Their physical descendants continue of course, but they are not the same type of souls as are those that have lived in the previous cycle. Those souls that developed that civilization and culture are no longer incarnate. They disappear from the earth, and leave their work unfinished. This is in every instance the case except in the case of those souls who have finished the work of the the cycle, and are therefore prepared for the next cycle or some subsequent cycle, in which case they incarnate in the cycle for which they are fitted. Of course we must guard against the mistake of assuming that each cycle is of a higher order than the one that preceded it. This is not the case at all. A very superior type of souls may live on the earth for a time and make way for a far less developed type. In the course of time, however, the turning of the Circles will bring back the cycle that produced the ancient civilization. The souls that will incarnate at that time will be the same souls that lived in the ancient time, with the exception of those who had grown beyond that stage, and with the addition of those later souls who have evolved to the point where they are ready for that cyclic type. Being in the main, the same souls, they will take up the thread of their work where they left it off when they were taken off the earth. In other words, they will pay no attention to the civilization that has been developed since, but having the same minds that they had before, they will at once commence a renaissance of their ancient civilization. Of course they will have forgotten much during their long absence from the earth, and hence the work of restoration will at first be rather difficult, but it is sure to be accomplished in the course of time.

Right here do we find the duty and the wisdom of building mighty memorials of our civilization and our culture. These must be of such a nature as to resist the ravages of time, and to continue until such time as the cycle shall be renewed. These memorials will be studied by the souls who lived at the time of their use, and in the course of time, owing to the fact that in the past these souls were familiar with them, their meaning will dawn upon the ones who study them. In this way will it be possible for the students to reconstruct the culture of the past. Thus, these memorials will be in the nature of books ,preserved through the ages, and handed to the ones able to decipher them. No one else will ever be able to read the message of the memorials. They can be understood only by the souls who were in ancient times familiar with their meaning. They are merely aids in recovering what one knew in the past.

Take as an illustration, the Monuments of
Mayax. They were a sealed book to the Span-
iards, and to all scientists, and they have been a
sealed book to the Mayas of modern times, who
are not the same souls as the Mayas who builded
the monuments. Finally Dr. Le Plongeon, the reincarnation of an old Maya who lived in Mayax
several thousand years ago, went to Yucatan and
there he was able to connect himself with his past,
and to recover much of the meaning contained in
those inscriptions. It was because of his famili-
arity with them in the past that he was able to
unveil the mystery of them. Why has his work
failed of recognition? Simply because this knowledge was for those souls of the ancient time who
had returned to seek fulfillment of their dreams,
and none but Mayan souls were entitled to this
knowledge. All such are accepting the work of
the Doctor, while the others scoff. Without exception, those who are looking into the lore or the
antiquities of the American Indians or the ancient
races of Mexico, are those souls from that time
who are now incarnate, and they discovered much
of the truth, while the real modern white man sees
nothing, for it is not for him. The Egyptologist
is in every instance the reincarnation of an ancient Egyptian soul and so all the way through.
In this way, the memorials of the past civilizations
are the connecting links which enable those souls
to reconstruct their former culture, when the cycle
returns and in that way begins to bring back the
souls of the original cycle. All the ruins that are
at this day a puzzle to so many, will in the course
of time be understood, when the time has come
for their message to live again. The question
may be asked, why is it that at this time there is
so much interest in everything connected with the

ancient civilizations     Simply because the original cycle has returned, and therefore, the souls of that time are incarnating again, and therefore they are collecting the data that they may restore their ancient civilization, seeing that they have no use for anything modern, as it is not suited for such souls.  Thus, there is nothing ever lost, all will reappear again when the time has come.

**For every birth of flesh ensouled, and of the fruit of seed, and every handiwork, though it decay, shall of necessity renew itself, both by the renovation of the Gods and by the turning-round of Nature's rhythmic wheel.**

The turning round of Nature's rhythmic wheel, or the turning or revolution of the Circles of the Heavens, acting in a purely natural way, and also the renovating influence of the Gods when the time of their several activities has arrived will cause all that has been in the past, and that has disappeared to come again into manifestation.  Every single birth of flesh, being ensouled, will have to come again when the time for its return has been reached.  They must all reincarnate and finish their work.  Death will not interfere with them. They may have been out of incarnation for thousands of years, but come again they surely will when their time has come.  This is not only true of men, but is also true of the souls of the extinct animals, when the cycle that produced them has returned again.  Every plant will come again when its cycle has returned, no matter for how many thousands or hundreds of thousands of years it has been extinct. Every handiwork of man, that has ever existed must of necessity

renew itself when the cycle to which it belonged
has returned. No matter how long they may have
decayed, they will all return when their cycle has
returned to earth once more. We often wonder
why it is that so much interest is being shown at
this time in the Philosophy and Religion of the
ancients. It is simply because those taking that
interest are those very same ancients who took
such interest in the ancient times. The teachers
who are seeking to get back the Ancient Mysteries
are those who in ancient times were Initiates of
the Mysteries. Those who are delving into the
Gnosis now, are those who trod the Old Old Path
in the years gone by. It is safe to say that those
who will truly understand and accept of the teaching in these Lessons will be the reincarnate souls
of those who in times past were Hermetic Scientists. All that was sacred to the ancients must be
restored again as those ancient souls return to
seek fulfillment of their dreams. As this cycle
progresses farther we will see more and more of
these evidences. These lessons are written for
our Brothers of the past who have returned to
earth as we have, they are not for the rabble of
the modern white race, who will never appreciate
them, but only for the souls of the ancients to
whom they belong. I write for Gentlemen, not
for Barbarians. This is the sense in which it is
true that there is nothing new under the sun, that
whatever has been, will be again, and that whatever is true of the present, has been true of the
past. The progress of science is in reality nothing more than the recovery of what has been lost
in the past.

For that whereas the Godhead is Nature's
ever-making-new-again the kosmic mixture,

Nature herself is also co-established in that Godhead.

The action of Nature on the cosmic mixture, which causes it to ever be made new again from its former state is what is termed the Godhead. It must be borne in mind that the revolution of the Cyclic Gods through the turning of the Wheel acts upon the cosmic mixture itself, so that it is transformed in an Alchemical manner, so that it is no longer suited to the original manifestations in Nature, but must manifest in an altogether different manner. This perpetual renewal of the cosmic mixture, following the Cyclic Law, constitutes the Godhead. At the same time, Nature is co-established in the Godhead, for the reason that Nature can operate only by using this cosmic mixture as the material for her operation. She will also find her operations circumscribed by the state of the cosmic mixture, so that she can only work out the quality of the cosmic mixture in the quality of the work which she performs. In this way, is there presented the great law of the inter-activity and the mutual reaction of Nature and the cosmic mixture the one on the other and through their conjunction and mutual opposition is brought into manifestation the process of Creative Evolution.

By making use of these principles is one able to become an Operative Hermetic Scientist. The Seven Secrets of the Great Work are to be found in this lesson, if the student is wise enough to interpret them correctly. They are: 1. the Protoplasmic Mixture of the Great Work or the First Matter of Art, 2. the ever-making-new-again of this mixture, 3. the Soul of the thing, 4. Reincarnation, 5. Death, 6. the Law of Cyclic Revolution, and 7. Cyclic Renewal. Add to these the process of Renovation, and the preserving of the fruits of the past achievements through the seeds which have been left behind, and you have all the steps in the Great Work. If you will preserve them in their continuity, you will be able to consummate the Great Work yourself, both within you and without you. This however will suffice for the wise, and the fools would never catch on, were I to perform the Great Work right under their noses. What has been said in this course of lessons will suffice as an Introduction to the Science of Alchemy, and this will be quite sufficient as an Introduction to the Gnosis of the Nature of all things. You are now ready to commence the study of the Hermetic Art, which will lead you directly into the Proana of the Temple of Alchemy and the Sacred Fire. Man, know thyself, and knowing thyself, thou wilt know all. Man, be thyself, and being thyself, thou wilt be all.

CPSIA information can be obtained at www.ICGtesting.com
Printed in the USA
BVOW02s1853301114

377281BV00004B/150/P